Eastern Oklahoma District Library System

EASTERN OKLAHOMA DISTRICT LIBRARY SYSTEM

3 3138 00951 9025

W9-CYY-063

Eufaula Memorial Library
301 S. FIRST STREET
EUFAULA, OK 74432

ALSO BY MICHAEL CORCORAN

For Which It Stands

Duel in the Sun

How to Break 90

Never Out of the Hole

The PGA TOUR Complete Book of Golf

The Golf Dictionary

THE GAME

OF THE

CENTURY

NEBRASKA VS. OKLAHOMA IN COLLEGE
FOOTBALL'S ULTIMATE BATTLE

MICHAEL CORCORAN

SIMON & SCHUSTER

NEW YORK   LONDON   TORONTO   SYDNEY

SIMON & SCHUSTER
Rockefeller Center
1230 Avenue of the Americas
New York, NY 10020

Copyright © 2004 by Michael Corcoran
All rights reserved,including the right of reproduction
in whole or in part in any form.

SIMON & SCHUSTER and colophon are registered trademarks
of Simon & Schuster, Inc.

For information about special discounts for bulk purchases,
please contact Simon & Schuster Special Sales at
1-800-456-6798 or business@simonandschuster.com

DESIGNED BY PAUL DIPPOLITO

Manufactured in the United States of America

1 3 5 7 9 10 8 6 4 2

Library of Congress Cataloging-in-Publication Data

Corcoran, Mike.
The game of the century : Nebraska vs. Oklahoma in college football's
ultimate battle / Michael Corcoran.
p. cm.
1. University of Nebraska—Lincoln—Football—History. 2. Nebraska
Cornhuskers (Football team)—History. 3. University of Oklahoma—
Football—History. 4. Oklahoma Sooners (Football team)—History.
5. Sports rivalries—United States—History. I. Title.
GV958.U53C67 2004
796.332'63'09782293—dc22   2004048719

ISBN 0-7432-3621-1

For Tommy, number 66 in my program,
and
Kevin and Kathleen, the number ones in his heart

Dear Old Nebraska U
(No Place Like Nebraska)

———

There is no place like Nebraska,
Dear old Nebraska U.
Where the girls are the fairest,
The boys are the squarest,
Of any old school that I knew.
There is no place like Nebraska,
Where they're all true blue.
We'll all stick together,
In all kinds of weather,
For dear old Nebraska U!

Boomer Sooner

Boomer Sooner, Boomer Sooner,
Boomer Sooner, Boomer Sooner,
Boomer Sooner, Boomer Sooner,
Boomer Sooner, OK-U!

Oklahoma, Oklahoma,
Oklahoma, Oklahoma,
Oklahoma, Oklahoma,
Oklahoma, OK-U!

I'm a Sooner born,
And a Sooner bred,
And when I die
I'll be Sooner dead!

Rah, Oklahoma! Rah, Oklahoma!
Rah, Oklahoma! OK-U!

Nebraska vs. Oklahoma, November 25, 1971

STARTING LINEUPS

Nebraska

OFFENSE

PLAYER	NUMBER	POSITION	WEIGHT
Woody Cox	32	split end	180
Daryl White	72	left tackle	238
Dick Rupert	77	left guard	221
Doug Dumler	54	center	237
Keith Wortman	65	right guard	238
Al Austin	78	right tackle	222
Jerry List	85	tight end	218
Jerry Tagge	14	quarterback	215
Jeff Kinney	35	I-back	210
Johnny Rodgers	20	split back	171
Bill Olds	44	fullback	215

DEFENSE

PLAYER	NUMBER	POSITION	WEIGHT
John Adkins	57	left end	221
Larry Jacobson	75	left tackle	250
Rich Glover	79	nose tackle	234
Bill Janssen	55	right tackle	228
Willie Harper	81	right end	207
Bob Terrio	45	linebacker	209
Jim Branch	51	linebacker	203
Dave Mason	25	monster back	199
Joe Blahak	27	cornerback	184
Jim Anderson	18	cornerback	180
Bill Kosch	24	safety	176

KICKERS

PLAYER	NUMBER	POSITION	WEIGHT
Jeff Hughes	26	punter	196
Rich Sanger	43	placekicker	214

Oklahoma

OFFENSE

PLAYER	NUMBER	POSITION	WEIGHT
Jon Harrison	12	split end	157
Dean Unruh	60	left tackle	235
Darryl Emmert	73	left guard	218
Tom Brahaney	54	center	231
Ken Jones	72	right guard	236
Robert Jensen	79	right tackle	244
Albert Chandler	82	tight end	234
Jack Mildren	11	quarterback	199
Leon Crosswhite	17	fullback	203
Joe Wylie	22	halfback	185
Greg Pruitt	30	halfback	176

DEFENSE

PLAYER	NUMBER	POSITION	WEIGHT
Raymond Hamilton	96	left end	237
Lucious Selmon	98	left tackle	221
Derland Moore	97	right tackle	252
Lionell Day	66	right end	236
Albert Qualls	81	linebacker	222
Steve Aycock	43	linebacker	205
Mark Driscoll	59	linebacker	208
Kenith Pope	28	cornerback	205
Steve O'Shaughnessy	18	cornerback	180
Larry Roach	26	safety	181
John Shelley	33	safety	195

KICKERS

PLAYER	NUMBER	POSITION	WEIGHT
Joe Wylie	22	punter	185
John Carroll	10	placekicker	205

Team Statistics for the Season, Prior to Game

	NEBRASKA	OPPONENTS
First downs	236	116
Rushing yardage	2,570	705
Passing yardage	1,839	1,012
Passes complete/thrown	141/242	99/232
Total points	389	64

	OKLAHOMA	OPPONENTS
First downs	227	171
Rushing yardage	4,333	1,627
Passing yardage	736	1,418
Passes complete/thrown	27/56	114/232
Total points	405	146

THE GAME
OF THE
CENTURY

ONE

It is not uncommon [in Nebraska] to see a rugged-looking fellow, who in any other setting wouldn't dream of wearing anything more daring than khaki, in bright red pants. [Red] is not a consensus expression of team spirit. It is a primitive form of biological adaptation. Just as leopards develop spots to blend in with the brush, Nebraskans wear red to blend in with their surroundings.

—Meghan Daum, a writer who had recently moved to Nebraska,
on National Public Radio's *Morning Edition*, July 13, 2001

IN THE LATE SUMMER OF 1859, JOHN KENDALL GILMAN and his younger brother, Jeremiah, were headed across Nebraska toward the Rocky Mountains in a wagon filled with goods to sell to miners. The Pike's Peak gold rush was in full boom, and the Gilman brothers were carting whiskey, tools, bullets, clothing, and nearly anything else a miner might spend money on, including one item that would be considered truly luxurious on the frontier: a water pump, made of iron and painted red. Pumps were a rarity; when a person wanted water from a well, a bucket was lowered using a hand-cranked windlass.

A few days' ride west of Fort Kearny, almost to the Colorado border, the axle on the Gilmans' wagon gave out near the bank of the Platte River. The brothers were stuck in the middle of nowhere, but they decided to make the best of it and settle on the very spot where the wagon broke down. They reasoned they could trade with the Sioux and Cheyenne in the area, as well as with emigrants heading west. If the Gilmans were going to stay put, they would need water, so they dug a well and installed the red pump. When they were finished they tied a tin cup to the pump so thirsty sojourners could take a drink. Thereafter the Gilmans built two sod houses and had themselves what pre–Civil War pioneers called a road ranch—a place to stop and make repairs, trade, buy mules or horses, and, most important, replenish supplies of food and water. The Gilman ranch became a noted landmark on the route to the far West, and the red pump in particular was a welcome sight to the weary. It became part of Nebraska legend.

Just a little over thirty years after the Gilmans set up their ranch—in 1892 to be precise—the University of Nebraska chose scarlet and cream as the school colors, thereby ensuring that whether it was the color of a water pump or a football jersey, red would forever by synonymous with Nebraska. At the time, of course, no living soul could envision a day eighty years later when the school's football team, known by then to Nebraskans one and all as Big Red, would be inextricably linked not only with the identity of the state as a whole, but also with the identity of nearly every single one of its citizens.

In 1970, Big Red shared the college football national championship with the University of Texas, and the 1971 Nebraska team looked to be the school's best ever. After a 41–13 drubbing of Oklahoma State in the seventh game of its 1971 season, the University of Nebraska Cornhusker football team was undefeated and, it appeared, unstoppable. The Husker defense had held opponents to a total of 40 points through twenty-eight quarters of play. During those same twenty-eight quarters, Nebraska's offense had scored 277 points. On October 30, Nebraska would face its most difficult game up to that point when it squared off against old rival the University of Colorado, ranked ninth in the country, in the nationally televised game of the week on the ABC network.

The output of the Husker offense was being matched by the farms that inspired the team nickname. The growing season had

been a good one, and now, the week of the Colorado game, it was
harvest time for corn. Near Bellwood, in Butler County (in the
eastern part of Nebraska, as is the state capital of Lincoln, where
Big Red plays its home games), brothers Gene and Jack Napler
stared out over their 415 acres of irrigated corn. The Napler
brothers were anticipating a yield of nearly 150 bushels per acre,
but they were preoccupied with the coming game. "We want to be
sure and get this harvest over so we can both be down at Lincoln
for the Colorado game," said forty-five-year-old Gene. The heavy
work during harvest would be done by the brothers' "Grow Big
Red" combine. Each of their three trucks (two large ones for
transport and one pickup) was red, and each bore a "Go Big Red—
Do It Again" bumper sticker. Gene had missed the Huskers' home
game against Minnesota earlier in the season because one of the
two brothers *had* to pick up some cattle. They flipped a coin, and
Jack went to Lincoln to see a 35–7 Big Red win. Gene went cattle
shopping.

"They kid us down at the elevator about having the fever bad,
but they sure are on the lookout for tickets," said Gene. "We listen
to the radio every morning to get the Nebraska ratings first and
the price of corn second. We know the price of corn will be down
because there's too darn much of it this year. But there is only one
Nebraska team, and it is number one."

Indeed, the Huskers were the number-one-ranked team in the
nation as they prepared to play Colorado, and if victory was to be
assured, no detail was too small to overlook. When Colorado
requested permission for its mascot, a real live buffalo named
Ralphie, to be allowed on the sidelines during the game at Lincoln's Memorial Stadium, Nebraska head coach Bob Devaney said
live animal mascots had no place on a football field. The only rep-
resentation of the mascot allowed would be a fifteen-pound
papier-mâché bison head worn by a Colorado coed.

There was no doubt that Martha Hill, the student wearing the
papier-mâché head, would be among the most discussed topics
before kickoff. For starters, she made it known she planned on

3

wearing brown hot pants and knee-high suede boots as she strutted her stuff before the 67,000 at Memorial Stadium. Women's liberation activists of the day may not have approved of her provocative (if one overlooked the gigantic head of a beast resting on her shoulders) dress, but Hill, a sophomore, was the first woman to be a human mascot at Colorado and said she "liked to be where the action is."

On the Saturdays when Big Red was at home, the action was in Lincoln. In later years, a popular bumper sticker emerged that read MEMORIAL STADIUM: THIRD LARGEST CITY IN NEBRASKA. Only the towns of Omaha and Lincoln offered a greater concentration of people than the football stadium during home games, a fact that was not lost on Ms. Hill, who was a graduate of Lincoln East High School. "I grew up loving football just like all Nebraskans," said Hill, "but I went west because I wanted to meet new people and do new, exciting things. Besides," she said with a wink, "I never could get tickets to the Nebraska games and this was one way to get into Memorial Stadium."

On the same day, October 23, that Nebraska traveled south for its road game against Oklahoma State, the University of Oklahoma Sooners headed north into Kansas for the sixth game of their season. With a 5–0 record, the Sooners were ranked second in the national polls behind Nebraska, and in the minds of many it was difficult to see how any team could be ranked ahead of Oklahoma. The previous year, stuck in a midseason rut, the Sooners had overhauled their offense and installed the triple-option wishbone attack conceived by University of Texas assistant coach Emory Bellard and first used by the Longhorns in 1968.

It was no coincidence that the wishbone was the ultimate running formation and that it was conceived and nurtured and had matured at the University of Texas. Darrell Royal, the Texas head coach who was a star quarterback at Oklahoma and captain of Bud Wilkinson's Sooners in 1949, believed the best way to move the ball was along the ground. "Only three things can happen when you throw the ball," Royal often said, "and two of them are bad."

4

When the wishbone was unveiled at Texas, opposing defenses reeled from the assault. After a tie with Houston to open the 1968 season, Texas lost to Texas Tech the following week, then ran off thirty consecutive victories over three seasons, including the national championship in 1969 and the shared national title with Nebraska in '70.

At 5–0 heading into the Kansas State game, Oklahoma's interpretation of the wishbone was clearly working, but the mind-numbing heights it reached on October 23, 1971, were incomprehensible. In the years to come after that day, when Oklahoma teams coached by Barry Switzer were winning national championships, writers and announcers fell in love with the metaphorical cliché that the Sooner wishbone swept over the opposition like a windblown prairie fire. If ever an offensive performance merited such flowery phrasing, it was the one against Kansas State. Oklahoma did not punt the ball once during the entire game, and scored touchdowns on its first *ten* possessions. The eleventh possession resulted in a lost fumble, and the twelfth in yet another touchdown. The final score was 75–28.

When Sooner star running back Greg Pruitt left the field near the end of the game, even the most diehard Kansas State fans rose to their feet to applaud what they had witnessed: In just nineteen carries, Pruitt had rushed for 298, breaking by 11 yards the Big Eight one-game record set by Gale Sayers in 1962. All totaled, the Oklahoma wishbone picked up 711 yards on the ground, or 66 yards more than the NCAA record at the time, and 36 first downs. Jack Mildren, the Sooner quarterback, rushed for 156 yards and threw just seven passes, completing four of them for a total of 74 yards. One of those passes was caught by Pruitt, who gained 34 yards on the play. "They are the greatest offensive running team I've ever seen," said Kansas State head coach Vince Gibson after the game. "I've never seen a better football team. Boy, they're great. I don't believe I've ever seen a better back than Greg Pruitt."

The Oklahoma wishbone wasn't so much a fire as it was an avalanche, and Greg Pruitt was not just some flashy running back.

He was a superb blocker, a fine receiver, and a smart football player who even played on punt-coverage teams. As Pruitt's fame grew, he took to wearing a particular T-shirt around the Oklahoma campus in Norman. On the front of the white shirt was the word OKLAHOMA and just underneath it was another word: HELLO.

The back of Pruitt's favorite shirt carried a single word: GOOD-BYE. It was a message to the defenses that Pruitt and the Sooners had yet to face.

When the Associated Press's weekly Top 20 poll was released on October 26, there were five other undefeated teams in the country: Georgia, Penn State, Auburn, Alabama, and Michigan. Nebraska still held the top spot in the poll with 31 first-place votes, but that was four fewer than the previous week. Oklahoma's record-shattering day against Kansas State made voters in the poll think twice about which team was number one, and the Sooners received 21 first-place votes.

For Oklahoma fans, the move toward the top of the national rankings was a welcome relief after several seasons that were, by Sooner standards, dismal. The school's football legacy was such that the feeling around the state was that the Sooners were on the way to restoring order in the football universe. At Nebraska, the football program had been building momentum since Devaney took charge in 1962. Even with the shared national title in 1970, however, Husker fans had yet to reach the point where (as they would in the not-too-distant future) they could view a national championship as a birthright.

With each passing week in 1971, college football aficionados around the country anticipated more and more the inevitable showdown that loomed between the Cornhuskers and the Sooners on November 25, Thanksgiving Day, in Norman, Oklahoma. It would, on every level, be the single most exciting and superbly played game ever in college football.

TWO

★

I do not remember crossing the Missouri River, or anything about the long day's journey through Nebraska. Probably by that time I had crossed so many rivers that I was dull to them. The only thing very noticeable about Nebraska was that it was still, all day long, Nebraska.

—Willa Cather, *My Ántonia*

AT THE END OF THE TWENTIETH CENTURY, THE members of the Associated Press in Nebraska voted on the state's top news stories of the 1900s. The Depression was voted the most significant thing to happen in the state during those hundred years, a belief that is hardly surprising. The economic crisis was combined with six years of drought and wrath-of-God-type dust storms that turned day into night by blotting out the light of the sun. Third on the list was the great blizzard of 1949, when it snowed for twenty-three consecutive days. The United States Army was needed to clear 87,073 miles of road and rescue more than 150,000 people from snowbound homes. Number six on the list was not so much a news event as it was the evolution of a state of mind: the overall success of Big Red.

That the Husker football team meant so much to Nebraskans was remarkable considering that the coach back in 1960, Bill Jennings, was so distraught over what had become a losing tradition that he was moved to say, "I've been watching things closely, and I

7

don't think this state can ever be great in anything. We can't feed the ego of the state of Nebraska with the football team."

Young men had been playing football at the University of Nebraska for seventy years when Jennings made his pronouncement. On Thanksgiving Day in 1890, Nebraska took on the Omaha YMCA and won 10–0. (At the time, a field goal was worth five points, a touchdown four, and the free kick after a touchdown was worth two points.) The Nebraska head coach, Dr. Langdon Frothingham, was a new teacher at the school who had come west from Harvard. Of all the things that qualify a man to be a football coach, Frothingham possessed the most essential—the ball itself. The reporter on the scene for the *Omaha World-Herald* wrote of the birth of what would become the Big Red Nation: "There were several hundred out to see the boys enjoy themselves and break each other's shins."

The reference to broken shins, if not strictly accurate, conveyed the rough-and-tumble nature of the game during its formative years. In fact, the sport of football was so violent that it was banned by some state legislatures and schools, and in 1906 a Nebraska player died during a game when he was flung to the ground by a Doane College player. Few, perhaps including the player himself, were aware that he'd suffered a concussion in a game versus Kansas the previous week. The incident was one of many that eventually (in 1905) compelled President Theodore Roosevelt to summon to the Oval Office the most influential minds in the game to ask them to play nice. Roosevelt did not (nor did he have the power to) threaten to ban the game entirely if his wishes were not heeded, and in truth, he loved the physical nature of the game. "I would rather see my boys play it," he said, "than to see them play any other game."

Frederic Remington, the renowned western artist, was even more adamant than the famously rugged Roosevelt. Remington said he found no merit in the "namby-pamby talk [regarding legislation against football], and hope[s] that the game will not be emasculated and robbed of its heroic qualities, which is its charm and its distinctive character." Remington suggested that those who found the game dangerous might instead find safety in a vigorous game of cards.

Nebraska and its people were the antithesis of namby-pamby, and football appealed to their willingness to work hard and persevere. The state's residents were of pioneer stock and knew the satisfaction that came from a job well done. Despite the later misgivings of Bill Jennings, football was *precisely* the type of thing that could bolster the ego of the citizens of Nebraska, a place where life itself was so hard that no game, no matter how violent, could seem too rugged.

Early Nebraska teams were often among the very best in the land, as were the coaches and players. In 1892, Nebraska beat Illinois for its first win over a major college, and the game's only touchdown was scored by George Flippin, a student who was among the first few blacks to play sports at any white university. Missouri later forfeited a game against Nebraska rather than take the field with a black man.

During the 1898 season, Fielding "Hurry Up" Yost coached the team. Yost later led Michigan to eight undefeated seasons in twenty-five years as head coach. It's impossible to say for certain, but Yost may have fled Nebraska to escape the team's string of ghastly nicknames. Originally known as the Old Gold Knights, the team's subsequent tries at a catchy handle included the Rattlesnake Boys, Tree Planters, Bugeaters, and Antelopes. The year after Yost left, Charles "Cy" Sherman, sports editor of the *Nebraska State Journal,* began calling the team the Cornhuskers. That name was sometimes used by Iowa's team, but the Iowa fans preferred another: the Hawkeyes. *Cornhuskers* was Nebraska's for the using, it seemed, and the name stuck, eventually becoming the official state nickname as well.

Under coach Bummy Booth, the Huskers won twenty-seven straight games from 1901 to 1904, including an '02 season when opponents failed to score a single point. The winning streak also laid the foundation for thirty-three consecutive home wins through the '06 season. "Nebraska occupies a unique position in western football," one newspaper reported in 1903. "Too strong to find fearful competitors, the Cornhuskers can almost weep with Alexander the Great because they have no more teams to conquer."

Still, back east, where the Ivies and Army ruled the game, it is unlikely many people were even aware Nebraska had a football team. Even Notre Dame was relatively unknown, but in a way, Notre Dame's rise to gridiron glory led to football followers in the East turning an eye toward Nebraska. In 1913, the Army team was considered unconquerable, and one of the best ever to play the game. Notre Dame was unheralded, a tiny Catholic school in Indiana with no discernible football tradition. That all changed when the two teams met and Notre Dame quarterback Gus Dorais and end Knute Rockne demonstrated the explosive potential of the forward pass. A rule change in 1912 lifted all restrictions against forward passing with two exceptions: Only one such pass could be made per four-down series, and the ball had to be thrown from at least five yards behind the line of scrimmage.

The new leniency that lent itself to heaving the ball downfield was ignored by nearly everyone except Dorais and Rockne. For certain, there had been forward passes thrown before the 1913 Army–Notre Dame game. As far back as 1876, as he was being tackled in a game against Princeton, Walter Camp of Yale had desperately heaved the ball forward to a teammate who scampered for a touchdown. (The referee was dumbfounded by the play, and in a Solomon-like manner, flipped a coin to determine if he would allow the play to stand. He allowed it, and Yale won the game.) Dorais and Rockne, however, were the first to integrate the pass into a game plan and to practice it with the full intention of using it. The resulting upset of Army put Notre Dame on the map and was the beginning of the Rockne legend.

Just two years later, Rockne was an assistant coach for Notre Dame as it prepared to play Nebraska for the first time. The Huskers were now coached by Jumbo Stiehm (pronounced *steam*) and were in the midst of an unbeaten streak that would eventually reach thirty-four games in 1916. Two years after the upset of Army, Notre Dame was still riding a tidal wave of newfound popularity when their train pulled into Lincoln for the game against the Stiehm Rollers. The Huskers' star ballcarrier was Guy Chamberlin, a lad from Blue Springs, due south of Lincoln not far from the state's border with Kansas. After scouting Nebraska, assistant coach Rockne informed the Notre Dame team not to lose any sleep over Chamberlin. He was a pedestrian runner who, Rockne told his team, "never cut back." On October 23, 1915, Chamberlin scored two touchdowns and the Huskers defeated mighty Notre Dame 20–19. Word went east along the wires to the big cities, and the *New York Times* described Nebraska as a team that had "come of age" and "must be ranked with the major powers." Chamberlin went down in history as one of the great runners of a decade that saw many, including Jim Thorpe.

The win over Notre Dame sparked a brief but intense rivalry that carried over into the Roaring Twenties, a golden age for college football that saw the emergence of Nebraska's first true superstar, two-time (1924 and '25) All-American Ed Weir. An undersized tackle who was the absolute definition of the All-American country boy, Weir hailed from Superior, a town about halfway across Nebraska's southern border with Kansas. Weir was a holy terror on the field, and in October 1923 he led the Huskers to a 24–0 victory in the first game in their brand-new Memorial Stadium. One month later on the same field, before what one newspaper called "the greatest crowd ever assembled in the Missouri Valley to witness a football game," Weir slammed the door on Rockne's soon-to-be-immortalized Four Horsemen in a 14–7 Nebraska victory. (The legendary backfield of Notre Dame's 1924 football team, the "Four Horsemen of Notre Dame," included quarterback Harry Stuhldreher, fullback Elmer Layden, and halfbacks Jim Crowley and Don Miller. They were so dubbed by sportswriter Grantland Rice in his account of the Notre Dame–Army game October 18, 1924, at the Polo Grounds in New York City: "Outlined against a blue-gray October sky, the Four

Horsemen rode again. In dramatic lore, they are known as famine, pestilence, destruction and death. These are only aliases. Their real names are Stuhldreher, Miller, Crowley and Layden.") Likewise, in the 1925 season opener in Champaign, Illinois, Weir and the Cornhuskers shut out the Illini and Red Grange, the practically mythical Galloping Ghost. Grange was an All-American halfback at the University of Illinois in 1923 and 1924. He was nicknamed the Galloping Ghost for his dazzling open-field runs, and became the first truly famous NFL star when he left school and joined the Chicago Bears in 1925.

The series with Notre Dame ended at the insistence of the Irish in 1925 because they felt they were treated in a shoddy manner by Nebraska whenever the games were in Lincoln. Taunted as "fish eaters" by the Nebraska crowds (an insipid attempt to insult the Catholic tradition of forgoing meat on Fridays and Holy Days) and once forced to use bales of hay for benches, Notre Dame left the Huskers off its schedule, but there were no lingering feelings of ill will between the two universities. In fact, Nebraska tried to lure Rockne away from Notre Dame to lead its own team. Rockne demurred, but did suggest a man with the most fantastic name in the history of coaching: Dana Xenophon Bible, the coach at Texas A&M.

Dana (or sometimes just D.X.) Bible often referenced the good book that provided him with his surname, and his teams defined glory by winning six Big Six titles from 1929 to 1936. His best team was the 1933 squad that went 8–1, losing only to Pittsburgh. Bible was earning $10,000 per year at Nebraska at the height of the Depression, surely making him one of the state's wealthiest residents. Still, after the '36 season, ol' D.X. decided the amount in the collection basket wasn't enough to keep him in Nebraska, and he vamoosed for Texas and a ten-year contract at $15,000 per annum.

The burgeoning Husker program fell into the hands of Biff Jones, a veteran coach who had led Louisiana State, Army, and Oklahoma. It was Jones's 1940 team that set the standard for

Huskermania for all the years prior to Devaney's arrival in 1962. On December 1, 1940, one day after finishing the season with eight consecutive wins after an opening loss to Minnesota, Stanford asked Nebraska to be its opponent in the Rose Bowl on New Year's Day. The Husker faithful were beside themselves at the news. After fifty years of playing football, Nebraska was finally going to a bowl game. For twenty-four hours, the students and people of Lincoln celebrated. Classes were canceled, and students rallied at the steps of the capitol, where they egged on the governor to lead them in rendition of the school song, "No Place Like Nebraska." The news that Nebraska was Rose Bowl–bound was, according to one local reporter, "the greatest thing that has happened to Nebraska since William Jennings Bryan ran for the presidency."

Of the thirty-nine football players who boarded a special train bound for California on December 19, 1940, thirty-eight were native Cornhuskers. At a stop in El Paso, Texas, the players crossed the border into Juarez, Mexico. Far from home and unaware of the oldest travel advice known to man, they drank the water, got sick, and were still feeling the effects when they lost to Stanford 21–13 in Pasadena. When the team made it back to Lincoln three days after the game, 2,000 people met the train at the station. It was cold and snowing, but that night 5,000 people showed up for a gigantic bonfire.

College football was still played once America entered the war at the end of 1941, and in many ways, especially at West Point and Annapolis, it was very important for the morale of the young men who took the fight to the Axis. At Nebraska, however, World War II meant the end of a good run for Husker football. The school had no military training programs to attract potential stud athletes that the military didn't get right off the bat. Even Biff Jones left for military service after a 4–5 season in 1941, the first of a string of losing seasons that didn't end until 1950. From 1941 through 1961, Nebraska's record was 72–125–4, and the team burned through eight coaches. Among those eight was Bob Devaney's immediate predecessor, Bill Jennings, and his "this state can never be great at anything" lamentations. Jennings resigned after a 3–6–1 record in 1961.

College football lore is thick with first-name-only coaching legends who ate nails for breakfast, exhorted their teams with squinty-eyed growls, and became lords of the region where their teams played, and owners of the hearts and minds of their players and followers. There was Bo and Bear and Woody and Ara and Knute, to name a few.

The man who reversed Nebraska football's decline toward oblivion had no thunder in his name. He was just Bob, and when he arrived in Lincoln in 1962, he could have easily been mistaken for someone in town for the day from Ohiowa, Shelby, Creston, Loup City, or a hundred other small towns in Nebraska. Bob Devaney *was* a football coach, but he looked more like a man who would give you an easy smile as he pushed his cap back slightly on his head and said he was sorry but your radiator was shot and that it'd be a day or two before the parts came in to fix it.

Devaney had a 35–10–5 record in five years as the head coach at the University of Wyoming when he left for Nebraska, but Wyoming football was not Alabama football, or Southern Cal or Oklahoma or Michigan football. People in Nebraska might have been hoping for miracles from Devaney, but no reasonable person actually *expected* them. To hear Devaney tell it, it was something of a wonder that he ended up being a coach at all. He studied economics at Alma College in Michigan, and when, in 1936, he hit the gridiron as a player for his first college game he promptly had three teeth knocked out.

After graduating from Alma, Devaney took a job teaching at Big Beaver High School in Birmingham, Michigan. Each day he taught six separate subjects, and after classes he coached. The teenagers at Big Beaver, Devaney said years later, "did not have much interest in athletics." The football team hadn't won a game in four seasons, and when he saw there weren't enough team members for a proper practice, Coach Devaney jumped right in and scrimmaged with them. There was no gym in which to practice basketball, so Devaney's wife, Phyllis, took a teaching job to buy a car so Coach Devaney could drive the basketball team to practice in another town. On a trip into nearby Detroit, the car was T-boned by a streetcar. "We weren't sly enough to pretend we were injured and sue the streetcar company for $50,000," said Devaney. "All we got out of it was $25 for the car."

In his own way, Devaney was learning how to be a coach, and the first thing he learned was that he didn't know much about coaching. He left Big Beaver for a job at Saginaw High School, still in Michigan, where he coached the baseball team, including a pitcher named Bob Buhl, who Devaney decreed didn't have much of an arm. Buhl was moved to first base, and later in life went on to become a mainstay of the pitching staff for the great Milwaukee Braves teams of the fifties. "Shows you what kind of baseball coach I was," said Devaney.

Still, along the way Devaney was getting the hang of coaching football, and as his teaching and coaching career drifted northward in Michigan, he became a winner. At Alpena High School, hard by Thunder Bay on Lake Huron, Devaney's teams won fifty-two games in sixty-one tries. He was thirty-seven years old and had been coaching high school football for fourteen years and, the way Devaney saw it, if he hadn't been home one summer day when the phone rang, that would have been the extent of his coaching career. "I was thirty-seven," said Devaney. "If a break didn't come my way before I was forty I was going to go back and get my master's and take a boring administrative job somewhere. I just happened to be in from the lake one day when [Michigan State coach] Duffy Daugherty called and my real life began. If he hadn't reached me, he'd have called somebody else. I have no illusions about that." Daughtery, the top assistant to State's Biggie Munn, offered Devaney a spot on the staff.

After four years as an assistant at Michigan State, Devaney was offered the top job at Wyoming in 1957. His self-effacing way and easy wit were excellent tools for recruiting athletes, but he realized the job held a unique challenge. The university was in Laramie, a midsize town in the least populated state in the United States. Once a teenager got a gander at the lack of bustle, it would be easy enough for him to spin around and get back on the bus or train or plane that brought him. So Devaney had his assistant coaches meet the recruits at the airports and bus terminals and train depots so they could put an arm around anyone who suddenly thought four years in Laramie might not be too cool.

"I learned to love Wyoming," Devaney said, but his stay there wasn't without its moments. Late one night on the road back to Laramie from a recruiting trip, Devaney dozed off and drove off the side of a cliff. "I thought I was driving hell out of it, too," said Devaney. "When we got to the bottom and I got out to look at the car I realized we'd rolled over three or four times." He told school administrators that a deer had dashed in front of him.

The night before one game, a player Devaney had recruited from New York was hanging out in the lobby of the hotel where the team was staying. A police officer who happened through thought the young fellow was loitering and asked to see some identification. The player refused, and some punches flew. Devaney and some of his assistants broke up the commotion, but they all ended up at the police station. "I offered a sound defense argument and about had it all straightened out," said Devaney. "Then I pressed my luck. They said the player had to spend the night in jail. I said, 'If he stays, we all stay.' So they locked us up. It was in the headlines the next day."

After five successful seasons in Laramie, Devaney headed east across the nearby border into Nebraska and all the way across the state to Lincoln. (Nebraska shares its borders with six states: To the north is South Dakota; to the east mostly Iowa and a little hunk of Missouri; there are two southern borders, so to speak. A straight line shared with Kansas runs east to west until it forms a northerly right angle at Colorado. That north-south part of the Colorado-Nebraska border goes on for about 120 miles until it hits the southeast edge of Wyoming.) He arrived in a town and state that had craved a winner for twenty hopeless years. While it was true that the 1954 team had gone 6–4 and been invited to the Orange Bowl because that game's rules forbade a second consecutive appearance by Oklahoma, Duke savaged the Huskers 34–7. Nebraska played so ineptly that the *Miami Daily News* reported the team "didn't belong on the Orange Bowl sod with Duke. It didn't belong on any bowl sod with anybody." The sting of embarrassment was felt throughout the state.

During the lean years, talk often turned fondly to the 1940 team and its Rose Bowl appearance. Devaney joked that people spoke so often and so enthusiastically about that game that he lived in Lincoln for several years before he realized Stanford won the game.

Before Devaney arrived, tickets to Husker home games were anyone's for the asking. The banks in Lincoln bought blocks of seats at Memorial Stadium and left the tickets on the counters for anyone to take free of charge. In other places around town and the state, game tickets could be had for fifty cents.

On November 3, 1962, Nebraska, under its new coach, lost a home game to Missouri, 16–7. Despite the loss, the Huskers were having a winning season and for the first time in as long as anyone could remember, every seat in Memorial Stadium was taken. It was the first in an NCAA record string of sold-out home games that has no end in sight as of this writing, more than forty years later.

The team finished the '62 season with an 8–2 record and a win in the Gotham Bowl over the University of Miami at Yankee Stadium. Despite 320 yards passing by Miami's George Mira, Nebraska won 36–34. After the game Devaney told his players they'd made him famous. "I've received a number of offers to give lectures on defense," said Devaney.

The Big Red Nation had been born.

Bob Brown was a physical giant in the days before young men routinely turned themselves into steroid-fed behemoths to play college and professional football. As a pro, Brown became a feared and dominating all-pro offensive lineman for the Philadelphia Eagles and Oakland Raiders. In the spring of 1962, he was a six-four, 269-pound tackle at Nebraska who was what players in a later era would call a "getover." Brown had a propensity for exaggerating the existence and extent of his injuries so he could skip practices, and was headed to the nowhere land that is home to supremely talented people who believe their gifts supersede the necessity to work hard.

Spring practice in college football is a time of year when players begin to stake their claims to positions vacated by the previous season's seniors. Based on his sheer size, Brown expected to be a starter in the fall of '62, and he was unmoved by the fact that spring practice represented his first chance to impress his brand-new coach. Devaney told the equipment manager to remove Brown's gear from his locker. When Brown found his locker empty, he sought out Devaney for an explanation. "I've been talking it over with the other coaches," said Devaney to Brown, "and we think it's best you give up contact sports. We recommend golf, or maybe tennis, where you can use your strength without getting hurt." Brown was stunned, and broke into tears while begging Devaney for another chance.

At the end of the 1962 season, Bob Brown was named an All–Big Eight selection. The following season he was named to the All-America team. Bob Devaney had a way with everyone, not just football players, and he succeeded at Nebraska where others had failed because his own view of life was in harmony with the place and the people.

After the winning season in '62, a writer spent time with Devaney to see what the man behind the renaissance was all about. The writer, from New York, was unimpressed. When he looked at Devaney he saw a frumpy man dressed in such impeccably bad and ill-fitting style that he compared the coach to Willy Loman. Devaney feigned fury over the story. "Tell that guy I'm going to sue him and his magazine for defamation," Devaney said. "Of course, he'll be able to offer the perfect defense—the truth."

Nebraskans saw something very familiar in Devaney. They saw a man who had spent cold nights on the high school sidelines along Lake Huron. They saw a man who stayed in town after he graduated from Alma, waiting tables and pumping gas so he could pay off $350 he still owed the college. Nebraskans could relate to the long road of struggle that led Devaney to them in his mid-forties because they were intimate with that road themselves. To Devaney, Nebraska was not someplace to be tolerated along the way to someplace else, nor was it a burden. He may not have realized it when he first arrived in Nebraska, but Devaney had found a home he would not leave until he passed away on May 9, 1997, at age eighty-two.

Bob and Phyllis Devaney moved into a modest house on a tree-lined street in Lincoln. Their number was listed in the phone book, and in the evenings the coach drank a bourbon and milk in his basement den. When a small college in Omaha put on a fashion and entertainment variety show, Devaney was there, preceded on stage by the Husker band's Sunshine Girl, who twirled a flaming baton. When Rotary Clubs wanted to liven up an evening, Devaney would stop by for a "Night with Bob Devaney." When the Omaha Symphony Guild wanted to create awareness for its annual fund-raiser, Devaney lent a hand, appearing at the kickoff to an exponentially increasing series of parties known as Symphony Football. For five dollars, Husker fans could and did subscribe to a regular in-season newsletter from the coach.

Most important, however, Devaney's teams won. The 1962 season was followed with records of 10–1 (Orange Bowl), 9–2 (Cotton Bowl), 10–1 (Orange Bowl), and 9–2 (Sugar Bowl). After five seasons and five consecutive bowl games, Devaney's record at Nebraska stood at 46–8. "Nebraska fans are understanding in defeat," he joked, "but I would not want to put them to a serious test." Despite his sense of humor, Devaney would soon be reminded that the thing that matters most to the majority of people in this world is what you've done for them lately.

THREE

Little by little the sky was darkened by the mixing dust, and carried it away. The wind grew stronger. The rain crust broke and the dust lifted up out of the fields and drove gray plumes into the air like sluggish smoke. The corn threshed the wind and made a dry, rushing sound. The finest dust did not settle back to earth now, but disappeared into the darkening sky.

The wind grew stronger, whisked under stones, carried up straws and old leaves, and even little clods, marking its course as it sailed across the fields. The air and sky darkened and through them the sun shone redly, and there was a raw sting in the air. During a night, the wind raced faster over the land, dug cunningly among the rootlets of the corn, and the corn fought the wind with its weakened leaves until the roots were freed by the prying wind and then each stalk settled wearily sideways toward the earth and pointed the direction of the wind.

—John Steinbeck, *The Grapes of Wrath*

WHILE BOB DEVANEY WAS BREATHING LIFE INTO A program that had been, for the most part, dead for twenty years, the University of Oklahoma was trying to rekindle a glorious post–World War II football run that energized the state itself, gave its citizens a much-needed reason to hold their heads high, and saw the Sooners become the most dominant force on the college football landscape.

Oklahoma's postwar legacy was born out of the Dust Bowl, the euphemism coined to describe the devastation wrought by the worst droughts in U.S. history. They were the same droughts that affected Nebraska during the 1930s, but that state's residents were spared the ignominy of being synonymous with the depths of human despair in America.

At its peak in the late thirties, the Dust Bowl consisted of 25,000 or so square miles in Kansas, Colorado, Wyoming, Texas, New Mexico, Nebraska, and Oklahoma. Much of the affected area had been plowed to grow grain during World War I (the much-lauded "breadbasket of democracy"), and doing so stripped the land of natural prairie grasses. When the rain didn't come and the wind did, the hardy roots of the prairie grasses weren't there to keep the topsoil in place. The rain didn't come, but prolonged strong winds did, and dust storms so powerful ravaged the land that the dust was carried all the way to the East Coast of the United States.

The dust storms imperiled life in all its forms. Crops withered and died, and breathing was difficult for humans and livestock. Folks made masks of bandannas so they could breathe, and those that had goggles wore them. Dust piled up inside houses and schools, worming its way through every crack. Banks foreclosed on farms. People fled for anywhere but here, and, legend has it, even the birds were afraid to fly.

Oklahomans had company in their misery, but for several reasons they alone became symbolic of downtrodden, Depression-era America. John Steinbeck's *The Grapes of Wrath* was a principal culprit in spreading the universal perception of the plight of the Okies, a dubious nickname Oklahomans came to loathe. Steinbeck had help from some of the most famous documentary photographs ever produced. Created by a group of U.S. government photographers, the images emphasized rural life and the negative impact of the Great Depression, farm mechanization, and the Dust Bowl. One of the most famous, shot in 1936 by Arthur Rothstein, showed a farmer and his two small sons in Cimarron County, Oklahoma, leaning into the wind as they walked past a shack during a dust storm. In the photo, the dust has piled up like snow around the structure. The boys' heads are level with its roof, and the tops of fence posts barely poke through the grit. The door of the shanty is only half visible above the top line of the dirt, giving the impression that the earth suddenly heaved up and swallowed the lower half of the structure. Cimarron County is in the narrow sliver of the Oklahoma panhandle, a part of the state that is just over thirty miles wide. The scene could just as easily have been photographed in Kansas or Texas, or New Mexico or Colorado, each within a stone's throw. But Rothstein hit the shutter button in Oklahoma, searing the image of the destitute Okies into the minds of people around the world.

In the small town of Hollis, tucked into the southwest corner of Oklahoma's non-Panhandle border with Texas, future Sooner quarterback Darrell Royal saw the crushing weight of a failed economy and nature impose itself upon his father, Burley. The elder Royal had been a farmer, but when the land died he picked up work where he found it as a truck driver, a sheriff's deputy, or a bookkeeper. Darrell, not even a teenager, asked his father where the Dust Bowl began and where it ended.

"Just stand there," said Burley Royal. "It'll find you."

There *was* football played at the University of Oklahoma before America entered World War II, and before the giant walls of dust, thousands upon thousands of feet high, made the world so dark that roosters no longer knew when to crow. In fact, students, teachers, and hangers-on at the college in Norman, just south of Oklahoma City, were playing football twelve years before the Oklahoma Territory was granted statehood.

The school's first football coach, John Harts, arrived in Norman for the fall term in 1895 to attend school and teach a class in elocution. He had been a student at Southwestern College in Winfield, Kansas, where he also played football. The idea for an Oklahoma football team was suggested by Harts at Bud Risinger's barber shop. Harts was the team captain as well as coach, but an injury he suffered in practice prevented him from playing in the first game. Short of players, Harts recruited the barber, Risinger, and a carriage driver to play in the school's first game. The team was defeated by students from a high school in Oklahoma City, and Harts retired with an 0–1 career record, then headed off to the Yukon to prospect for gold.

When the school's first full-time coach first laid eyes on Norman, he was underwhelmed. "A searing wind blew great dust clouds from the southwest," wrote Vernon Parrington in 1897, "as I stepped off the train and started for the university. I passed through a stretch of burnt-up slovenly village, and out along a quarter-mile of plank walk—the very nails of which were partly drawn out by the heat—and at last came to the university grounds, a small patch of brown prairie with a single red brick building topped off with a wartlike cupola."

Vernon Parrington had played at Harvard, and taught his football charges at Oklahoma the game as it was played in Cambridge. That is to say he taught them the mass-momentum plays, wedge formations, and cross-blocking that defined eastern football, and even taught students and other fans how to cheer in an organized fashion. Dressed in tweeds, Parrington followed his team up and down the windswept field and occasionally rolled himself a cigarette. On New Year's Eve in his first season, Parrington's team faced off against Kingfisher College at the fairgrounds in Guthrie, the territory's capital north of Oklahoma City. Early in the game, Oklahoma end Bill McCutcheon was being pounded by a Kingfisher player. "He hurt me every time he hit me," McCutcheon later said. It was little wonder—underneath his shirt the Kingfisher tackle had an elbow of stovepipe over each shoulder and his upper arms. Down at halftime, Oklahoma rallied to win, but not before the Logan County sheriff intervened in what he thought was a donnybrook. The sheriff had never seen a football game in progress before, and once he was sufficiently convinced he was witnessing good, clean fun, he announced the recommencement of play by firing his revolver into the sky.

Over four autumns, Parrington compiled a 9–2–1 record, then stepped aside as coach to focus on teaching. He remained as athletic director, but was eventually fired in 1908, along with twenty-two others including university president David Ross Boyd, in the shift of political power that accompanied statehood—the new governor refused to renew the contracts of all Republicans on staff. On the recommendation of Boyd, Parrington was immediately snatched up to join the faculty at the University of Washington. It was during his time there that Parrington wrote the two-volume *Main Currents in American Thought,* the first in-depth look at American literature and ideas, for which he was awarded a Pulitzer Prize in 1928.

Around the time that Parrington, Boyd, and the others were given the boot, the team became known as the Sooners, a nickname that harked back to the series of land rushes that established the Oklahoma Territory starting in 1889. One of the few rules for claiming land was that all participants wait for a cannon shot before starting their mad dash. Those who abided by the rule were called Boomers, for the sound the cannon made. Those who refused to be restrained from land-ownership by the existence of a silly rule struck out early, i.e., sooner than was allowed. They were called Sooners. Oklahoma's early football teams were known as both Rough Riders and Boomers for ten years before the university borrowed the permanent name from a school pep club called the Sooner Rooters.

In 1905, Parrington hired Bennie Owen to coach the Oklahoma team. Owen was quite literally a Sooner: At the age of seventeen, he took part in the famous Cherokee Strip land rush from the south Kansas border into Oklahoma Indian territory. His age prevented acquisition of any land, but his sense of adventure took him four miles into the territory before he turned back.

Bennie Owen had a genuine football pedigree. He played and coached under Fielding Yost at Kansas and Michigan, quarterbacking ol' Hurry Up's offense. As a play was coming to its conclusion, Owen would bark out the signals for the next play from the bottom of the pile. He weighed a mere 126 pounds, but he was a fighter, and as coach of Oklahoma Owen did more than anyone else to establish the tradition of the Sooner program.

Early in the 1907 season, Owen lost an arm to a hunting accident, an occurrence that might have forced a lesser man to step down as coach. After recovering, Owen returned to coach the Sooners in 1908 and stayed longer than any coach in school history. Four of Owen's teams—in 1911, 1915, 1918, and 1920—were undefeated, primarily because Owen was the first coach at a big school to fully incorporate the forward pass into his overall offensive scheme.

At the end of the 1920 season, Owen announced that he intended to raise money to build a new football stadium. On October 20, 1923, the first game was played on the site of the stadium-in-waiting, and in 1925, the first contest was played in front of the new stands on the west side of the field. The 16,000-seat stadium cost $293,000 to build and was named Oklahoma Memorial Stadium to honor university-associated persons who died in World War I. Stands were added to the east side of the stadium in time for the 1929 season, raising total seating to 32,000. By that time, Owen had been retired from coaching for three years. He was still the athletic director, however, and even though the structure was called Memorial Stadium, the turf upon which the Sooners trod came to be known as Owen Field.

The years after the opening of Memorial Stadium were the times of the Depression and the the Dust Bowl, followed by world war. In the wake of that procession of chaos, and for the most part because of it, Oklahoma football would rise up and take the citizenry of the state along with it.

Oklahomans believed that John Steinbeck's most famous novel visited terrible opprobrium upon them, and so *The Grapes of Wrath* was banned in some school districts in the state. But just as one of Steinbeck's fictional characters who wore a gold football on his chain represented hope to the Joads, there were nonfiction characters in the state who felt that the citizens of Oklahoma would find a renewed sense of being in Sooner football. Those men, all moneyed professionals of one sort or another, met with University of Oklahoma President George Lynn Cross and university regent Lloyd Noble on the school's campus in January 1946.

Cross opened the meeting by saying, "Every man in this room knows why we are here. The war is over and our state's upside down. We must make sure that this does not translate into a downward spiral for this university."

Noble added that "the problem is Steinbeck's damn book."

Cross got to the point. "There is only one way to get this state back on track, and that's football, football, football." The heads of lawyers and doctors and oil tycoons nodded in agreement.

Football, in all its forms, had been used as an analogy for various aspects of life as long as men had been kicking a ball along the ground or scooping it up and running with it. In his epic poem *The Lord of the Isles* (1815), which culminates in the famous battle at Bannockburn in 1314 between outnumbered Scots, led by Robert the Bruce, and the English, Sir Walter Scott wrote:

> Then strip, lads, and to it
> though sharp be the weather,
> And if, by mischance, you should
> happen to fall,
> There are worse things in life
> than a tumble on the heather,
> And life is itself but
> a game of football.

As the distinctive American form of the game evolved in the nineteenth and early twentieth centuries, there was no letup in the "football is life" analogies. "The game of college football is to college life what color is to a painting," said Bob Zuppke, who coached the University of Illinois from 1913 to 1941. "It makes college life throb and vibrate." To celebrate the end of World War I and inspire traders in November 1918, Charlie Brickley of Harvard drop-kicked a football across Wall Street and into the waiting arms of Jack Gates, a Yale man, who stood on the balcony of the New York Stock Exchange. The game could elicit powerful emotions in fans, and coaches knew if they struck the proper emotional chord with their players it could lead a team to realize its potential. From Rockne's "Gipper" halftime speech to a beleaguered Irish team, to Yale's Herman Hickman reciting *Spartacus to the Gladiators* ("Ye call me chief, and ye do well to call me chief. If ye are men, follow me!") before a game with Harvard, the search for a fresh angle to tap into the adrenaline supply of a team was endless. What Cross was suggesting to the men in that room in January 1946 was that a winning Sooner football team could help the people of Oklahoma realize *their* potential—that the game could transition from being analogous to life to literally being the thing that gave people a reason to believe.

Cross and Oklahoma athletic director Jap Haskell believed that the road to Sooner victories would be paved with the best of the abundance of rugged and incredibly fit football players exiting the military. A coach familiar with the various teams and players that had sprung up in the military during the war was needed. Haskell had served in the navy with Jim Tatum, and knew that Tatum was the head coach at the University of North Carolina before the war, and that he'd coached a navy team in Jacksonville, Florida, and served as assistant for the team at the navy preflight training program at Iowa under Don Faurot. Coach Faurot was the pioneer of an offense known as the Split T when he coached at the University of Missouri prior to the war. The two were soon assigned a young assistant coach name Charles Wilkinson, who arrived at Iowa after serving as deck officer on the USS *Enterprise* during the landings at Iwo Jima and Okinawa. Wilkinson was enamored with the Split T.

Tatum, a gruff, unkempt fellow, was hired as the new Sooner head coach (chosen over Bear Bryant, among others) and brought

28

951-9025

Wilkinson along with him. Temporarily relaxed recruiting regulations and the will of Cross presented Tatum with a virtual carte blanche, and he took advantage of it. Tatum and Wilkinson looked high and low for men returned from service overseas who had played for other colleges before the war. They raided other colleges for talent and snatched up every high school whiz they spotted. The new head coach was intent on breaking the will of and running off every member of the war-weakened 1945 team, and for the most part he succeeded. Tatum held tryouts, winter practices, spring practices, and summer practices. It is believed that six hundred players were herded into Tatum's football factory, nine of whom eventually made All-America. In the process, Tatum was burning through cash: The athletic department's surplus of $125,000 was gone before the first game of the 1946 season, and the team ran up an additional deficit of $113,000 during the season.

The '46 season was a promising start toward Cross's eventual goal. Operating out of the Split T, the Sooners ran up an 8–3 record, and pounced on North Carolina State in the Gator Bowl. Privately, however, Cross thought Tatum too rough around the edges to be the personality the state would rally around, and was secretly delighted when he learned the University of Maryland offered Tatum its head coaching job. When Cross saw the ultimate Sooner coach in his mind's eye, it was not Tatum he pictured, but Wilkinson. Charles "Bud" Wilkinson was tall, handsome, and urbane. He held a master's degree in English from Syracuse University, played the organ, and read classical literature to unwind— an overall dashing figure. When Tatum left for Maryland, Wilkinson was immediately promoted to head coach and a dynasty was born at Oklahoma.

Wilkinson's voracious mind fed on the possibilities of the Split T. "The team in possession of the ball," he said, "knows when the play will start and where it will go. The defense must adapt to the movements of the offense. The value of the initiative cannot be stressed strongly enough. In exploiting the initiative gained by possession of the ball the offense can accomplish the minor objec-

Eastern Oklahoma District Library System

tives which lead to eventual touchdowns. If it is possible to build an offense that grinds out a steady succession of short gains, gradual gains in field position will result. In addition to field position, such a style of attack allows a team to keep possession of the ball longer, because short steady gains result in more first downs. Possession of the ball is the best defensive tactic in the game. The opponents cannot score when they do not have the ball."

While most teams favored the very tight single-wing formation, Wilkinson knew the Split T employed wider splits along the offensive line, which in turn spread the defense along a wider front. The wider defensive front was more susceptible to straight-ahead runs of the backs in the Split T, who because of their own wide splits weren't forced to hit the line at angles or take any looping steps. The biggest advantage to the Split T was that it hit the defense in the mouth right from the snap. In the single wing, the ball was shoveled back several yards behind the line of scrimmage (what is today known as a shotgun formation) and all the ball fakes took place behind the line; then the ball had to be advanced back to the line. The quarterback in the Split T took the ball under center and moved directly and laterally along the scrimmage line—the ball never went backward. All the fakes took place along the line, so no time was wasted, in essence creating a quicker strike at a foe who had less time to react. Wilkinson boiled it down to "speed while hitting over a broad front, with all the fakes along the line of scrimmage and the constant threat of a forward pass." If that pass was thrown, it was a jump pass thrown right at the line, or a ball heaved on the run as the quarterback rolled toward the sideline.

Working the sidelines in a crisp white shirt and neatly knotted tie, Wilkinson even made other coaching legends feel self-conscious. "Bud always looks like he just stepped out of a barber shop," said Bear Bryant. "I wish I had his class." Ara Parseghian felt likewise. "Bud was my idol," said Parseghian, "and I felt uncomfortable looking across the field at him."

Wilkinson had a voice that was as smooth as his style, but he never raised it. He was not a sideline lunatic in the manner of Woody Hayes. Beneath the calm, however, his players knew there was no compromise. The building blocks of victory, he preached, were the desire to win and physical conditioning. All football coaches expect desire and hard work from their players—few get it and even fewer have the ability to draw it forth from players in the manner Wilkinson did. The will to win came first because without it "athletes seldom pay the price to get in top condition," said Wilkinson. Asked to describe the will to win, Wilkinson recalled the 1950 Big Seven championship game versus Nebraska, a game his team won 49–35. The game's best-remembered play came early in the second half when Billy Vessels, a Sooner halfback, scored on a 67-yard run. It wasn't until the next day, while watching film of the game, that Wilkinson and his staff noticed the most astonishing effort they'd ever seen in a single play. The play was an end run to the right side of the line. Fullback Leon Heath, wearing jersey number 40, was assigned to hook-block the Nebraska left end in toward the center of the line. The defender came upfield so quickly, however, that Heath was forced to drive him toward the sidelines and create a lane for Vessels to cut up inside. When Vessels made his cut, he slowed down momentarily to avoid a Nebraska lineman, and as he did so set himself up to be blindsided by a Husker linebacker. The Sooner staff watched in disbelief as Heath flashed across their movie screen and wiped out the approaching linebacker. In the clear now, Vessels cut back against the grain toward the opposite sideline. After running 40 yards downfield, Vessels ran out of room when a Husker cornerback achieved an angle on him and forced him to the sideline. Suddenly, out of nowhere, Heath appeared *again* and leveled a devastating block on the lone defender. Vessels scored standing up, all three key blocks on the play thrown by the same player. "The physical effort involved in blocking three men," said Wilkinson, "and moving 96 yards at a sprint to get at the three opponents is something that cannot be accomplished by anyone who does not have the desire to play everything to the hilt. Unless a team possesses more of this quality than the opponent, it is virtually impossible for superior technical football to prevail."

Wilkinson took the thoroughbreds he'd assembled with Tatum and never looked back. When the military recruits graduated, he built his teams around schoolboys from within a self-imposed 150-mile radius of campus. Players such as Darrell Royal, an Okie from the Dust Bowl, and others who came from Texas, anchored the Sooners. By the end of the 1949 season, Wilkinson's third, he was in New York at Gene Leone's restaurant to receive the national coach of the year award from the Scripps-Howard newspapers. Former president Herbert Hoover was among those who gave him a standing ovation. Wilkinson's team hadn't lost since the second game of the 1948 season and the streak would last 31 games. As amazing as that was, an even longer streak followed. A 16–4–2 run served as an interlude between the 31-game victory streak and the incomprehensible 47–0 mark that began in 1953 and didn't end until a 7–0 loss to Notre Dame in 1957. It is an incontestable fact that Bud Wilkinson's Sooner teams from 1948 through 1957 produced the single greatest prolonged stretch of dominating play in college football history, with an aggregate record of 94–4–2. They were national champions in 1950, 1955, and 1956, providing the kind of pride of place that Cross had set out to create. Oklahoma did not lose in an astounding 74 straight conference games from 1946 to 1959 (72–0–2), a streak that ended with a loss to Nebraska.

During halftime speeches, Wilkinson eschewed the typical rah-rah approach and instead sought to motivate his men with the words of historical titans. Sometimes it was the old First Fan himself, Theodore Roosevelt. Sometimes Shakespeare. Another favorite was Winston Churchill, and while it wasn't apparent at the time, the loss to Nebraska in 1959 was, as Churchill put it after the Battle of Britain, the end of the beginning—albeit a beginning that lasted thirteen seasons. The Sooners had a losing record for the first time under Wilkinson in 1960 (3–6–1) and won only a single conference championship in his last four indifferent seasons.

In 1964, Wilkinson resigned as head coach to run for the U.S. Senate as a Republican. For one of the rare times in his life, Wilkinson picked the losing side, and after being swept aside as a candidate in the avalanche that crushed Barry Goldwater's run for the presidency, he more or less drifted off into the sunset. He left behind a football constituency that knew winning like no other, a feeling that had been summed up best by Cross in 1950 when he appeared before the Oklahoma state legislature to explain why the university needed twice the budget the governor had recommended. Cross later recalled that as he finished his thirty-minute oration "a sleepy-looking senator just to my right on the front row, raised his hand and said: 'Yes, I'd like to ask the good doctor why he thinks he needs so much money to run the University of Oklahoma.'"

"I would like," responded Cross, "to build a university of which the football team could be proud." The assembly had a good chuckle at that one, but the smiles were few in the seasons after Wilkinson departed the Sooners.

During all the wins and winning streaks and championships during the seventeen-season Wilkinson era at Oklahoma, Gomer Jones coached the Sooner linemen. At a time when the big eaters played both sides of the ball, Jones tutored sixteen All-Americans. He had joined Wilkinson's staff in 1947, after coaching the line at Nebraska for a season after the war. As did Wilkinson after serving in the navy, Jones spent time coaching a service team. When Wilkinson quit to run for the Senate, it seemed a natural transition to hand off his legacy to his most trusted and beloved lieutenant. Gomer Jones led the Sooners for two seasons. The '64 squad's record of 6–4–1 looked sterling compared to the 3–7 record in

1965. The demand to produce a winner was too much for Jones, and he stepped aside as coach after two seasons while remaining as athletic director.

The void left at the top of college football by the decline of the Sooners had been filled by the University of Alabama and the man passed over in favor of Jim Tatum, Paul "Bear" Bryant. The Crimson Tide won the national championship in 1961 and '64, and shared it with Michigan State in 1965. All that Wilkinson had wrought was crumbling at Oklahoma, and even though Wilkinson himself led the search for the right candidate to replace Jones, there were no takers at first. The Sooner faithful were unanimous in whom they wanted to coach the team: Darrell Royal. He was, as the school's fight song goes, Sooner born and bred, and despite the successful program he was building at the home of the archenemy University of Texas (the Longhorns were national champions in 1963), the feeling was that any Sooner legend who had played for Wilkinson would leap at the opportunity to be the Oklahoma head coach. Royal declined, as did the University of Georgia coach Vince Dooley, and the University of Tennessee's Doug Dickey.

It was time for one dynasty creator to call another, Wilkinson decided, and he dialed up Bryant at Alabama. Could the Bear recommend one of his assistants, Wilkinson inquired, or perhaps even a former player? "I can't think of anybody," growled Bryant.

Soon after the phone call ended, Bryant did think of someone, and he called Wilkinson back with a name: Jim Mackenzie.

Wilkinson knew who Jim Mackenzie was even if Sooner fans didn't. Mackenzie was a lineman on Bryant's University of Kentucky team that had snapped Wilkinson's first big winning streak. It was in the 1951 Sugar Bowl, in what would have been victory number thirty-two in a row, that Kentucky whipped the national champion Sooners 13–7.

When Mackenzie got the call from Wilkinson in December 1965, he was preparing the defense of the University of Arkansas Razorbacks for their upcoming Sugar Bowl appearance versus Louisiana State. Mackenzie was being wooed by the University of

Maryland as well, but he wanted to coach the Sooners. "It's the best job in America," Mackenzie told his wife, Sue, and soon it was his job.

One of Mackenzie's first priorities was to convince future Heisman Trophy winner and state schoolboy hero Steve Owens to sign with the Sooners. Owens had always dreamed of playing for the Sooners, but there was a hitch: Mackenzie had recruited Owens for Arkansas by saying, "You don't want to go to Oklahoma because you don't want to be part of a rebuilding situation." After he was hired by Oklahoma, Mackenzie sent assistant coach Galen Hall to see Owens in Miami, a town in the far northeast corner of the state. The message to Owens was "Never mind what was said before. We need you to come and help bring Oklahoma football back to where it belongs. Besides, it's where you've wanted to be all along."

But Owens hesitated, and Hall called Mackenzie, who jumped in his car and drove seven hours on ice- and snow-covered roads to close the deal. There was still another hitch: Owens and the other joint holder of the state high school player of the year award, Rick Baldridge, had promised each other they would go to the same school.

"Rick just told me he's coming to Oklahoma," Mackenzie told Owens.

"He did?" said Owens. "Then I am, too."

The next time Owens saw Baldridge he learned Mackenzie had used the same trick with him. Whatever the method, it kept Owens from going to Arkansas.

Even if Mackenzie wasn't Royal, he was highly regarded by his peers. His head coach at Arkansas, Frank Broyles, called Mackenzie an "outstanding coach. He had charisma, mystique, everything you needed to be very, very successful." The talent of the assistant coaches who joined him at Oklahoma was immense: Galen Hall, Chuck Fairbanks, Barry Switzer, Jimmy Johnson, and Pat James would all one day be among the very best head coaches in the college and professional ranks.

"I love being a head coach," Mackenzie said to his wife after they moved to Norman. "I love making decisions. I even love deciding how many shoelaces to order."

The 1966 Sooners started the season 4–0 and were ranked tenth in the country when number one Notre Dame paid a visit to Norman. The Irish had twelve All-Americans, notably defensive tackle Alan Page, and won in a massacre, 38–0. At season's end, the Sooners were 6–4, but even those fans who initially doubted Mackenzie's ability to turn the program around saw plenty to be optimistic about. A total of ten more points spread out in the right places over the course of the season, and the Sooners would have been 9–1 instead of 6–4. Furthermore, the hated rival, Texas, and Nebraska had both been defeated. Mackenzie was named coach of the year in the Big Eight, and his players loved him.

"I don't want to give the wrong impression," said Owens, "because [Mackenzie] was great to me. But he was an imposing guy. There was no bullshit about him, and he expected people to do more than they thought they could." Mackenzie never yelled at players during a game, because he thought it distracted them from the job at hand. During practices, however, he would lay into his troops. In the strategic sense, some felt Mackenzie was a downright brilliant Xs and Os man, better than even Bryant himself. He made a habit of scribbling his notes and philosophies on coaching on scraps of paper and on the back of play diagrams.

Mackenzie stood 6 feet 2 inches and the frame that made him the scourge of the Sooners as a Kentucky player often carried as much as 260 pounds when he was a coach. He smoked filterless Camels, sometimes two, three, or four packs a day. He slept just a few hours each night and thought little of driving all night to visit a recruit.

In April 1967, Mackenzie poked his head in Switzer's office at the university. The head coach was like an older brother to Switzer, who had played and coached at Arkansas and followed Mackenzie to Oklahoma with Broyles's blessing. Mackenzie was leaving to

drive to western Texas to recruit a star schoolboy. "Don't run anybody off while I'm gone," Mackenzie joked to Switzer as he left.

"That was the last time I saw him alive," Switzer said.

Mackenzie, just thirty-seven years old, had a fatal heart attack
in his home in the middle of the night after returning from the
recruiting trip.

FOUR

★

Then we lost our sixth game to Keene State . . .

—caption on a cartoon hanging on the wall of Bob Devaney's
office at Nebraska in the summer of 1971. In it, two bums
sitting on a sidewalk swap tales of better days.

WHEN BUD WILKINSON HIT THE RUBBER-CHICKEN
circuit as Oklahoma's head coach in 1947, he was fond of saying
the "first important thing I learned about coaching was that a
coach needs more than a couple of funny stories."

Bob Devaney never wanted for a funny story. One of his
favorites was about a series of phone calls from Bear Bryant. After
a 10–0 regular season in 1965, Devaney took his Huskers to Miami
to play Bryant's Alabama team in the Orange Bowl. Bryant's boys
thrashed Nebraska, 39–28. "The next year," said Devaney, "Coach
Bryant called again after the regular season and said, 'Let's get
together and have some more fun, Bob.'" So Devaney took his 9–1
team to the Sugar Bowl and they got creamed again by 'Bama,
34–7. "A few years later," said Devaney, "Bryant called again suggesting we get together again in a bowl game. I said, 'Which bowl
do you have in mind, Bear?'"

"We were thinking about the Liberty Bowl," said Bryant.

"I said, 'Gee, that sounds great,'" said Devaney. "And the next
day we signed to go to the Sun Bowl."

The ability to laugh in the face of adversity was one of

39

Devaney's most admirable traits, but he was a football coach first and foremost, and he felt a sting from the lopsided losses to Alabama at the end of the '65 and '66 seasons. The Alabama teams weren't as big or strong overall as the Nebraska teams they beat, but they were faster, and Devaney realized the winning trend in college football was toward more and more speed. In order to keep the Huskers near the top of the football food chain, Devaney and his staff would have to combine the bruising style of their early teams with a faster-paced attack and swifter athletes.

Devaney knew that the prospect of change creates emotional extremes in people, and that the nerves of sports fans were particularly prickly when it came to upheaval surrounding their teams. When Devaney took over the Huskers in 1962, the fans were desperate for change. The new coach was eager to acknowledge that desire, and on the first play of the first game in Lincoln, aware that the Huskers rarely threw the ball downfield, Devaney called for a pass. It was his message to the red legions that things were going to be different from that point on. The crowd went bonkers with delight at the sight of the ball hurtling through the air. Ralph Beechner, who handled the public address microphone at Memorial Stadium for thirty years, was asked upon stepping down in 1971 to recall his fondest memories of game days in Lincoln. The first play he mentioned was the opening pass in Devaney's first home game, ten years prior. "He called a pass play and the fans simply went wild," said Beechner. The profound and lingering impact the play had on fans is truly remarkable, because the pass was incomplete.

With that one play Devaney won over the hearts of Nebraskans. He knew that when fans are accustomed to losing, change is perceived as good. After being swamped by Alabama in the Sugar Bowl on New Year's Day 1967, Devaney realized the necessary changes weren't as simple as throwing a single pass. Nobody hates losing as much as people accustomed to winning, and as the 1967 season approached, the expectations of Cornhusker fans were at the point where the next logical steps in the progression of success were undefeated seasons followed by major bowl game victories and national championships. What they got instead were back-to-back seasons of mediocrity as the Huskers finished 6–4 in 1967 and '68. Quickly forgotten was the fact that Devaney had rescued the Husker program at the brink of oblivion. Full-blown grumbling and second-guessing commenced, followed by the drumbeat of opinion that Devaney should be fired. "You could see the pressure building on Devaney," said George Sullivan, the team trainer at the time.

"There were rumblings that people wanted to get rid of Coach Devaney," said Boyd Epley, who was a student and pole-vaulter on the Nebraska track team at the time, and who, in a fortuitous twist of fate, would end up helping Devaney right his listing football team.

The nadir of Devaney's years at Nebraska came on November 23, 1968. In the final game of a forgettable season, the Huskers were humiliated by Oklahoma, 47–0. In the aftermath of the pummeling, Devaney, ever the salesman, looked desperately for a way to make lemonade out of a lemon of a situation. "If we have any kind of people coming back next year," Devaney said, "this should make them quite determined not to let anything like this happen again."

The 47–0 win over Nebraska in 1968 was the highlight of an otherwise pedestrian 7–4 season for the once mighty Sooners of Oklahoma and their young head coach, Chuck Fairbanks. Youth and lack of head coaching experience were never viewed as a drawback to holding the top job at Oklahoma because university president George Cross possessed an uncanny knack for knowing a winner when he laid eyes on one. Wilkinson had been just thirty when he started as head coach, and Mackenzie was thirty-six when he took on the job. Fairbanks was thirty-three when George Cross asked him to lead the Sooners after Mackenzie's death, and had been an assistant at the school for just one year.

Nearly forty years after his first year season as Oklahoma head coach, Fairbanks recalled his early days at the school. "I was a defensive coach for [Jim Mackenzie] that first year. Homer Rice was on that staff with us, and he left after the '66 season to become head coach at the University of Cincinnati. After Homer left, I became Jim's offensive coordinator as we started preparation for the '67 season. Jim died of a heart attack during spring practice. Let me tell you something—Jim Mackenzie was really special. Following in his footsteps was not easy. But I was at such a great school, and had such good assistant coaches. Barry Switzer was there at the time as a young coach who didn't realize he was as good a coach as he actually was. I made him offensive coordinator and he didn't want to take it; he didn't think he'd know what to do. Pat James was one of the best defensive coaches I've ever been around.

"We had good coaches, and a great president in Dr. George Cross," said Fairbanks. "If you could create a college president you'd like to have going into a situation like that, it'd be Dr. Cross. He set the mold for a president who was supportive of intercollegiate athletics in the right way. He loved it, he watched it, he was there, he went to practices, went to games. I couldn't have had a president who was more supportive during my young inexperienced days in college."

The fact that Fairbanks's coaching staff was one of the most substantial collections of football minds ever assembled was living proof of one of Mackenzie's coaching maxims: *Form a team of winners. Surround yourself with players and people to whom football means a lot.*

Mackenzie's habit of scribbling his thoughts on bits of paper and the backs of play diagrams left an ersatz thesis of his coaching philosophy for those who came after him. After Mackenzie died, Fairbanks looked through the coach's desk and found the scraps of wisdom. Fairbanks edited the pile down to twenty concise points on coaching and added the heading "The Winning Edge" before giving them to the rest of the staff. "I never knew another coach like Jim," said Fairbanks. "He had such a good feel for the game. He knew that a game boils down to a few important plays. He could just see it happening and tell the players, 'Now is the time to capitalize.'"

Among other elements of "The Winning Edge," Fairbanks listed these:

- Don't coach caution into good players.
- Look for and recognize your mistakes in coaching.
- Only players can win games, but poor coaching can lose them.
- Be yourself, not an actor. Players recognize phonies.
- Make second effort part of your personality.
- The kicking game is one-third of football, and it is the phase of the game where the big breaks occur.
- Prepare for the psychological lifts and letdowns.

Inspired and put in place by Mackenzie, the 1967 Sooners recorded a 10–1 record. In large part, the coaches realized they were just looking after what Mackenzie had started. "Same coaches, same players, same scheme," said Barry Switzer. "We all knew whose team it was." Nonetheless, it was Fairbanks who had to lead the team going forward. The memory of Mackenzie got credit for the winning season in '67, but when the brilliant seasons stopped it would be Fairbanks who shouldered the blame. The 7–4 season of '68 that included the ambush of Nebraska was followed by a 6–4 season in 1969. The blow of the lackluster '69 season was softened when senior Steve Owens won the Heisman Trophy, but when the 1970 season got off to a wobbly 2–1 start for the Sooners, everything was not OK in Oklahoma. The brilliance of the coaching staff notwithstanding, Sooner fans were greatly dissatisfied after a loss to Oregon State at Owen Field, and the hugely meaningful annual rivalry game with the mighty Texas Longhorns lay dead ahead. The sentiment of most Oklahomans regarding the Sooner head coach was summed up in two words that started popping up on bumper stickers, window signs, and even signs placed on the front lawn of the Fairbankses' home: "Chuck Chuck."

As a collegian, Fairbanks had played for Biggie Munn on Michigan State's 1952 national championship team. "I was a tight end and outside linebacker," said Fairbanks. "We had a lot of success as a team and had a twenty-eight-game winning streak under Biggie Munn and Duffy Daugherty. My position coach was Bob Devaney. Bob was a great coach and friend."

After his days as a player ended, Fairbanks stayed on at Michigan State as a student coach. "We had a whole bunch of coaches come out of Michigan State in that era," said Fairbanks. "Back in the seventies they called us the Michigan State Mafia because so many of us came out of that program." Along with Devaney and Fairbanks, future head coaches such as Frank Kush, Bill Yeoman, Dan Devine, and George Perles also did their apprenticeships at Michigan State.

As it had been with Devaney, Fairbanks's coaching took shape on the high school fields of Michigan. In Fairbanks's case it was at Ishpeming High, in the western part of the state's upper peninsula. "I coached high school in Michigan for three seasons after I left Michigan State," said Fairbanks. "Then I was an assistant coach to Frank Kush for four years at Arizona State. Then I was the offensive coordinator for Bill Yeoman at the University of Houston for four years before I went to Oklahoma with Jim Mackenzie."

The parallels between Fairbanks and Devaney didn't end with Michigan roots and ties to Biggie Munn. Both men were about to have their immediate futures altered by the suggestion of an assistant coach that would lead to strategic changes in the offensive schemes of their respective teams. It had been a phone call from Daugherty on Munn's behalf that landed Devaney at Michigan State, where he coached Fairbanks. At the pivotal moment of Fairbanks's coaching career at Oklahoma, it would be a middle-of-the-night phone call *to* Munn that reassured him that a decision he was about to make was the right one. That decision would lead directly to the best college football game of the twentieth century.

Tom Osborne joined the Nebraska coaching staff as a graduate assistant in 1962, Bob Devaney's first year as head coach. Osborne personified the state of Nebraska. He was a sincere and stoic man, courteous and well-mannered, who combined great intelligence with the knowledge that the best way to get something done was to put your shoulder to it without complaining. His personality was shaped in large part by the war years. When his father went off to fight, Osborne was four, and he, his younger brother, and his mother moved in with her parents in St. Paul, a small town ninety miles or so northwest of Lincoln. Banks had foreclosed on two separate farms owned by the grandparents during the Depression. Osborne's father was away from the family for five years during the war, and his absence and the general uncertainty of the times created a sense of being "from the wrong side of the tracks," said Osborne. As a result, Osborne felt his life was "directed toward proving something."

Osborne played high school football in Hastings, a midsize (by Nebraska standards) town a few hours' drive southwest of Lincoln, and played some more at Hastings College before spending three modestly successful seasons in the NFL with the Washington Redskins and San Francisco 49ers. Osborne was practical enough to realize that he didn't have an especially promising future in professional ball, so he decided to pursue a graduate degree in educational psychology at the University of Nebraska, where Devaney added him to the staff as a grad assistant.

Years later, when Osborne was the head coach of Nebraska, his wife, Nancy, remarked, "I've often thought that Tom belongs to a generation gone by, from a time when the West was won. There was a time when a handshake meant a deal was done, when a man was measured by his actions, not by what he said. Tom doesn't say much, but when he does, he really has something to say."

By 1969, when he was coaching the receivers as a full-blown member of Devaney's staff, Osborne had something to say about the dismal performance of the Nebraska offense the previous two seasons. The full-house backfield that was the basis of the Husker offense was too limiting, Osborne thought, so he suggested to Devaney that they organize the Nebraska attack around a two-back I formation that offered the opportunity to combine a crunching ground attack with play-action passing and more diverse play calling overall.

Searching for any source of energy to move his team out of the doldrums, Devaney agreed to Osborne's suggestion. In the twilight of his life, reflecting on the success that followed, Devaney said, "I'd like to say I turned it around, but it was Tom."

Early in the 1969 season, Osborne made another suggestion to Devaney that may have struck the old coach as a bit eccentric since it involved team members following the lead of a pole-vaulter with an injured back. "I wouldn't say I was a track *star*," said Boyd Epley, thirty-four years after the day he became the Nebraska football team's first strength coach. "I was a scholarship pole-vaulter and I did hold the school record, but I was disappointing. My career never got to the point where I would be considered a star.

"One day I missed the pit, landed on the runway, and hurt my back," continued Epley. "So I went into the weight room to strengthen it. The weight room was just a small space off of the training room with one Universal gym and five dumbbells. There was one bar with 390 pounds of weight plates, and one bench. That was it. The football players who couldn't practice because they were injured would hang around in there, but they didn't really have a strength-training regimen. They saw me working out and I guess I looked like I knew what I was doing. Pretty soon there were several of them waiting for me to show up every day so they could follow me around and do my routine.

"I can't remember the exact routine I was doing at that point," continued Epley. "The thing is, as a pole-vaulter I was looking for the same kind of explosive power football players need. To be able to sprint forty yards with a pole that creates resistance requires training that produces results similar to those the football players were looking for—great acceleration and the strength to power

46

down the field. When you're pole-vaulting and you run down there and stick the pole into that box buried in the ground you're going from a horizontal action to a vertical action. There is a great impact—like running into a brick wall almost. You need strength to do that.

"So," said Epley, "I took lifting seriously and the athletes who played football saw that and they wanted to use a similar approach to training. It wasn't long before Tom Osborne called me. I wasn't sure what to say when the trainer came in the weight room and said, 'There's a phone call for you.' So I went into his office and the voice on the other end was Tom Osborne. He said, 'Are you the guy who has been showing these players how to lift weights?' I wasn't sure what to say at that point because I thought maybe I was in trouble. He asked me if I'd come to his office."

Epley was hardly prepared for what happened next. "When I got over to Osborne's office," said Epley, "Cletus Fischer, the offensive line coach, was there with him. They both said how impressed they were with the players who'd been lifting weights, and how they'd returned to practice from their injuries with superior strength. Coach Osborne asked if I could do that for the entire team.

"I said, 'I'm just a student like they are.'"

"We understand that," said Osborne. "But can you do it?"

"I guess I can," said Epley, "but you don't have enough equipment and the room is too small."

"Well," said Osborne, "we were kind of counting on you to tell us what we need."

The next day Epley was in Osborne's office with a list of the necessary equipment. Osborne handed the list to a secretary and told her to order it. If it was that simple, thought Epley, why not ask for more?

"Coach," said Epley, "I forgot the second page of my list. Can I bring that tomorrow?"

Osborne laughed and gave Epley an understanding wink. Epley returned with a list half as long as the original list.

"*Now* is this everything we need?" asked Osborne.

"Yes," said Epley.

"Good," said Osborne. "Now we need to go in and talk to Coach Devaney. We need to make him aware of what we're going to try to do here."

Presently, Epley was standing in front of Devaney. "I found myself trying to explain why Nebraska needed a strength program for the very first time," said Epley. "Here I was in front of Bob Devaney and I was just a student. But Coach Osborne told Devaney he thought it was a good idea that the players lifted weights. He had seen some of the improvements they had made and he felt I might be able to help the whole team."

"Why?" asked Devaney. "None of the other schools are doing it. My friend Duffy Daugherty at Michigan State, his players don't lift weights. Why should we?"

"It will help your players get faster and they'll get stronger, too," said Epley.

The prevailing wisdom among football coaches at the time was that players who lifted weights would get slower, and even the best athletes were actively discouraged from using weights. Devaney looked Epley square in the eye and said, "I trust Tom and I think he's maybe on to something here, but I don't want to force the players to do it. We'll let them do it if they want to. But if any of them get slower, you're fired."

"I hadn't even been hired yet," said Epley years later, "and I was already threatened to be fired. I wasn't even an employee! But to have the head coach tell me that motivated me. He had a great sense of humor, but when you picked up the phone and he was on the other end there was always a little fear because he was a very intense man. I didn't want to let him down."

That Devaney was willing to try the weight-lifting plan at all demonstrated how sharply he still felt the effects of the devastating 47–0 loss to Oklahoma at the end of the previous season. "That game was on national television when not many games were," said Epley. "It was very embarrassing for Coach Devaney and he was looking for anything that would turn the program around. So when Coach Osborne made the suggestion, he went along with it. If they hadn't lost so bad to Oklahoma he might not have agreed to try something so drastic, and in those days it was considered drastic to lift weights. People made fun of you if you lifted weights, like you were odd or something."

Perhaps Devaney was thinking of the stigma associated with weight lifting when he told Osborne and Epley that he wouldn't force players to participate. If that was the case, Epley reckoned, he would have to find a carrot to lure the players into the weight room. "I approached the physical education department," said Epley, "and asked if we could create a class where these football players who wanted to lift weights could actually register for a class rather than have them just wander into the weight room. I wanted a little more structure. I wanted the players to be more accountable, because if they didn't improve I was done and Coach Osborne would be embarrassed and the whole thing would have been for nothing.

"The players weren't very strong," said Epley. "We didn't have a single player who could bench press three hundred pounds. It takes years to develop strength. Most of them were natural athletes, and athletes just didn't lift weights back then. We were the first school to lift weights in-season since Billy Cannon played at LSU in the fifties. A weight lifter named Alvin Roy showed Cannon what to do. I'm not sure they kept it going after Cannon left.

"We created two weight-lifting classes, and future All-Americans like Rich Glover, Larry Jacobson, and Jeff Kinney were in them. Every one of them got faster and stronger, and after the season was over Coach Devaney was so pleased he tripled my salary to three thousand dollars."

With a new offense and players becoming stronger and faster by the week, Devaney struck gold in 1969. "We played Oklahoma in Oklahoma and beat them 44–14," said Epley. "It was the most lopsided loss in their history on their field. In one year we turned it around from 47–0 to 44–14. Our players were stronger than they had been the year before. They still weren't *strong,* but they were stronger."

The thumping delivered to Oklahoma at Owen Field fueled the cries in Norman to "Chuck Chuck."

Meanwhile, the equilibrium was restored in Huskerland when Big Red capped off a 9–2 season in 1969 by pulverizing Georgia 45–6 in the Sun Bowl game that Devaney used as the punch line to his joke about the phone calls with Bear Bryant.

FIVE

Tomorrow to fresh woods and pastures new.

—final line of John Milton's poem
Lycidas, written in 1638

AROUND 1825, THE ORIGINAL DUKE OF WELLINGTON
(General Arthur Wellesley), hero of Waterloo, was visiting his old
secondary school at Eton when he spotted a cricket match under
way. "The battle of Waterloo was won on the playing fields of
Eton," the Iron Duke is purported to have said. Some historians
dispute whether it indeed was Wellington who said the words,
since it is known he held no great affection for Eton or his time
there as a young man, and the famous line wasn't attributed to
him until 1889, nearly forty years after his death. Nonetheless,
the words echoed across a century and around the globe, and are
often reached for when some coach or athletic director desires to
explain the deeper role sports play in shaping the character of
young people.

Wellington may just as well have been inspired by watching a
game of football, a sport which was then making the transition
from an unruly pursuit enjoyed by the great unwashed to a pas-
time of young gentlemen at famed secondary schools such as Eton
and Harrow. It was at a lesser-known school in the rural borough
of Rugby, in central England in Warwick on Avon, that the seed
was planted for the American version of the game.

Among the countless other things the Romans brought with them while conquering Britain in the second century B.C. was a game called *mellay*. The game that inspired the modern English word "melee" involved kicking or throwing an object across a goal line while opponents employed any preventive tactic that came to mind. The ball in early games was often the decapitated head of a defeated enemy. Mellay became an expected part of medieval festivals and even, in the town of Chester, a tradition used to mark Shrove Tuesday and the time when villagers had formed a human wedge and drove from their midst the Roman soldiers who used their town as a camp (or *castra*, hence the town's name). Over time, mellays pitted teams from different towns against one another, and the skulls of slain pirates and other misfits were replaced with the inflated bladders of pigs and, eventually, balls fashioned by local cobblers from animal hides. The game itself was a mass of confusion and violence, and through the centuries, including the early ninteenth when it appeared on the playing fields of Eton and Harrow, it was an anything-goes affair save for one clear rule: The ball could not be carried in the hands and arms.

The fateful moment that shaped the baseline concept of American football occurred in 1823, during a football game at the secondary school in Rugby. The end of such games was traditionally marked by the bells tolling five. One afternoon, a student named William Webb Ellis was on the receiving end of a long kick. His team was behind and Ellis no doubt sensed the five o'clock bells were imminent when he did something unprecedented: He caught the ball and ran like the dickens toward the other team's goal. The other players were bewildered, and hesitated before giving chase, no doubt with the idea of tackling Ellis. But Ellis was not to be caught, and even though his goal was disallowed, he had started something.

It wasn't until 1968 that would-be tacklers looked at each other as hopelessly as those who watched Ellis's mad dash down the field at Rugby.

In the summer of 1968, Emory Bellard was in his office at the University of Texas watching film of West Texas State running the two-back veer-option attack, an offense that was very much in vogue. "We had three great running backs at the time," said Bellard, "and I wanted to find a way to get them all in the game at the same time."

As Bellard watched the 16 mm film in the dark, the projector whirred and dust drifted across the shaft of light that carried the black-and-white images of tiny football players through the air until they came to life on the screen. In the days before videotape, a football coach's strategic ideas were formed in company with the mesmerizing hum of the projector, the coach inevitably leaning closer and closer toward the images as if the secrets of the game might be revealed to him if he became one with the film. In his hand, Bellard held a directional controller connected to the projector by a black cord. When the black button on top of the controller was depressed, the projector rewound, and the football players who had just completed a play on the screen flew off the ground and ran backward to the line of scrimmage. When Bellard let the button go, the players ran the same play again, over and over.

What Bellard saw time and time again was that after the West Texas State quarterback faked to the fullback (who plunged through the line and looked for a linebacker to block), there was no lead blocker for the quarterback and the pitch man as they tried to flank the defense on the outside edge of the scrimmage line.

Bellard reasoned that if he put all three Texas running backs in the backfield at the same time he could create the ultimate triple-option formation by positioning the fullback closer to the quarterback than the two halfbacks. The result looked like this:

O [QB]

O [FB]

[HB] O   O [HB]

"The best way to run the triple option was an alignment that had the two halfbacks deeper than the fullback for a good pitch path from the quarterback," said Bellard. "That way you can get the pitch man to the corner faster and have the lead blocker [the other halfback] close to the pitch man." In other words if the play went to the right, the right halfback was the lead blocker and the left half-back was the pitch man, i.e., the third option. The first option was a handoff to the fullback, who plunged into the line on every play. The second option was that the quarterback kept the ball and turned upfield if the defenders with the responsibility of preventing the defense from being flanked ("contain" in footballspeak) over-committed to denying the pitch.

Bellard asked some former Texas players to help him demonstrate the new concept to his boss, the Sooner playing legend and Longhorn coaching legend Darrell Royal. During the demonstration "I played quarterback," said Bellard, "because I was the only one who knew what he had to do."

As soon as Royal saw the formation it reminded him of the Split T he ran during his All-American days as Oklahoma's quarterback. "It's a good, sound method of running the ball," said Royal in later years. "And it damn near causes people to commit everything to stopping the running game, so it opens up some great throwing opportunities. The quarterbacks who are good at it are blacksmith types. They can't be running the ball out of bounds because they're afraid of getting hit." Royal thought about calling the new set the Y formation but a sportswriter from Houston, Mickey Herskowitz, gave it a name that stuck: the wishbone.

Starting with the third game of the 1968 season, Texas won thirty consecutive games until a loss to Notre Dame ended the streak in the Cotton Bowl on New Year's Day 1971. By that time the Longhorns had been the undisputed national champions in 1969 and been named the 1970 national champions in the United Press International coaches' poll conducted before the bowl games were played. In one game against Southern Methodist University in 1969, *four* different Texas backs rushed for more than 100 yards.

While Texas flourished, Oklahoma floundered. The Sooners had a load of hot young players in Norman thanks to the recruiting success of the coaching staff, but as the 1970 season opened the team was attempting to run an offense, the Houston veer, that didn't suit the talent the Sooners had on hand. "From the time I became head coach through the 1969 season, we ran out of the I formation based around the strength of Steve Owens," said Fairbanks. "It was right for us, and he won the Heisman Trophy for us, but after he left we didn't have any real I-formation power."

When the '69 season ended, Fairbanks and his staff began working with the team to install the veer offense created by Bill Yeoman at the University of Houston. Yeoman was Fairbanks's boss at Houston and part of the Michigan State Mafia. "We thought we could run the veer offense, which was a triple-option offense," said Fairbanks. "It was the offense we had run when I was the offensive coordinator at Houston. Bill Yeoman did more than anyone else to bring the triple option into college football. He learned it from Colonel [Red] Blaik at West Point, and then he taught it to me. The veer was predicated on an efficient passing game. It required first and foremost that you throw the ball effectively so opponents would be forced to defend the pass first. Once they were determined to defend against the pass, then you could run the triple option."

The decision to run the pass-dependent veer offense was not a bonehead decision on the part of Fairbanks and his two chief offensive assistants, Barry Switzer and Galen Hall. They had every reason to believe they could be a very proficient passing team based on the presence of junior quarterback Jack Mildren in their lineup.

Larry Jack Mildren, born in 1949 in Kingsville, Texas, was practically a mythical figure in Texas and Oklahoma. In the autumn of 1967, during his senior year at Cooper High School in Abilene, Texas, Mildren threw for 2,076 yards and 20 touchdowns, most of them to a speedy end named Jon Harrison. When he wasn't throwing, Mildren was running for 787 yards and *another* 24 touch-downs. Mildren's incredible numbers merited all-universe consideration viewed in the context of high school football in West Texas.

"Cooper was a new school on the south side of a town that was historically very good in football," said Mildren. "To wit, in the 1950s Abilene High won fifty-some-odd games in a row, a national high school record. It was a town that *cared* about its high school football games on Friday night. And the new high school had struggled for a while until we were all ninth-graders and a new coach, Merrill Green, came to town. From that point onward, the new school kind of took over from a football perspective. District Two had two schools in Midland, two schools in Odessa, a school in San Angelo, one in Big Spring, and two in Abilene. When I was a junior we played at Odessa Permian in front of 18,000 people. The next season, we beat them in Abilene. It was a district regarded by college scouts as a place where there was no question that the guys could play major college football. It was simply a question of where they'd play it.

"My senior season," continued Mildren, "we were 13–1. Didn't lose until the state championship game. We had a number of guys get scholarships. Three guys from our team went to SMU. Johnny Harrison and I headed north."

Jack Mildren's senior season at Abilene Cooper got the attention of every college football coach in America. He wasn't merely a promising recruit; he was *the* recruit, the player every school wanted, the prize high school prospect in all the land.

"I'd never been in an airplane before," said Mildren. "And that was a memorable thing in my life. Dan Jenkins ended up writing an article about my recruitment for their [*Sports Illustrated*'s] football preview in 1968. My dad talked to him a lot. I liked the town and campus in Norman. My dad had been a high school coach, and we drove to Norman and to some other campuses during the summer to see what they were like when the band didn't meet you at the hotel. I liked Barry Switzer and Chuck Fairbanks, and that was

56

important. My family was very comfortable with the football part and the academic part. I originally wanted to be an accountant, but that didn't last too long. I ended up majoring in petroleum land management. Some people have a pretty vivid imagination about what happens to you when you cross the Red River [from Texas into Oklahoma], but I wasn't the first, nor would I be the last. West Texas is still fertile ground for the Sooners. Switzer also spent a lot of time recruiting Johnny Harrison. There's no question that if we hadn't been teammates, Jon still could have played anywhere. We weren't recruited as a package."

Harrison, who goes by Jon but whose coaches and teammates from high school and college to this day refer to him as Johnny, didn't follow Mildren directly to the University of Oklahoma. "I went to junior college," said Harrison. "It was a grades thing, and I wasn't real comfortable taking entrance tests. I wasn't a great high school student. I wasn't a very good tester. I never flunked anything in high school, but just got kind of Cs and Bs. I don't remember my class rank, but it wasn't very high. Jack and I weren't the kind of friends that did everything together in high school. I was more of a wallflower than Jack. I was quiet and really didn't do a whole lot, didn't have a car in high school or anything like that. But we kept in touch when we went to college.

"I was recruited by three Southwest Conference teams," said Harrison, "Texas, SMU, and [Texas] Tech. Since Jack went to Oklahoma, I was recruited by Oklahoma, too. NEO [Northeastern A&M] won the national [junior college] championship when I was a senior in high school. That's in Miami [Oklahoma], up near Joplin [Missouri]. So I thought that'd be a good place to go. And we ended up winning the national championship my sophomore year. I wanted to go to OU, and when they got Jack they were going to run a veer offense, which meant there would be two wide receivers. That was sort of new, and I thought I had a better chance there than I did at other schools. Most teams didn't throw the ball a whole lot back then."

Under NCAA rules, college freshmen were ineligible for varsity competition prior to the 1972 football season. At Oklahoma, the freshman team was known as the Boomers, and like freshmen at every other college, they played a limited schedule and occasionally scrimmaged the varsity reserves. The low-key nature of freshman football changed dramatically when Jack Mildren rode into Norman in 1968 at the head of a superb class that included Oklahoma's schoolboy player of the year, running back Roy Bell, and linebacker Steve Aycock and defensive back Steve O'Shaughnessey. The question on the minds of Sooner fans everywhere was, "How good is Jack Mildren?" The hoped-for answer was that he was the one who would lead the Sooners back to the promised land.

On October 14, 1968, a Monday night, Mildren led the Boomers onto Owen Field for a game against the freshmen from the University of Kansas. In the stands, unbelievably, were *20,000* people, all on hand to see the future. Mildren threw for 346 yards and Bell scored two touchdowns. The Boomers won 55–20, and suddenly were the talk of the town. That didn't sit well with the Sooner varsity squad, who two days before had dropped to 1–2 with a 26–20 loss to Texas. "I'll never forget this," said Mildren laughing. "The student paper published an article that the freshmen ought to play out the remainder of the schedule for the varsity. You can imagine how popular that made us in the locker room. *Tense* is not a strong enough word to describe it. On Mondays when we [freshmen] didn't have games, we would scrimmage the varsity guys who didn't play in the game the preceding Saturday. Owen Field just had minimal lighting for practice because there were no night [varsity] games. Anyway, you know in the fall it gets dark early, and we'd be in a goal-line scrimmage around dusk and, you know, it's really a question of who's the toughest, the freshmen or the varsity guys? And I'd get under center and look up at the defense and start counting guys . . . ten, eleven, twelve, thirteen . . . hey, wait a minute! The varsity guys kind of wanted to bring it on to the freshmen. It was a little testy for a while."

When the Boomers played Texas Tech in Lubbock, people in

Abilene chartered buses to make the 300-mile round trip to see Mildren, their hometown star, in action. The Boomers won, 34–18, and followed with a 77–7 victory over Tulsa. Then came a showdown with Oklahoma State and its touted freshman star, Dick Graham. The game was telecast across the entire state by WKY-TV, and 14,000 spectators showed up at Owen Field. The Boomers won 28–21. Just twenty-three seconds remained on the clock when Mildren scored the winning touchdown with a 7-yard run.

Monday night thrills continued right into 1969 with perhaps the most talented overall freshman class ever to hit Oklahoma up to that point. Players such as Joe Wylie, Greg Pruitt, Dean Unruh, Tom Brahaney, Derland Moore, Albert Chandler, Raymond Hamilton, and Leon Crosswhite would be part of the core of the team that faced Nebraska in 1971. On one memorable night in 1969, the Boomers were locked in a 20–20 tie with Kansas at Owen Field. The 9,000 spectators on hand let the officials know loudly and clearly that they felt a call had been blown. The hootin' and hollerin' was so loud that Kansas players couldn't hear their quarterback call the signals, and the referee penalized the Boomers. Predictably, this set the fans off even more, and fired up the Boomers. Leon Crosswhite intercepted a pass, and on the very next play Joe Wylie hustled 86 yards for a touchdown.

Both the 1968 and '69 Boomers finished their four-game seasons unbeaten, stoking the fires of expectation. At the varsity level, 1969 was Heisman winner Steve Owens's team, but with his departure the Sooner faithful looked to Jack Mildren to lead in 1970. The epiphany that the Houston veer wasn't going to return Oklahoma to glory came after the third game of the 1970 season. "We determined early on in the 1970 season that we weren't as good as we needed to be passing the ball to successfully run the veer," said Fairbanks.

"Jack *was* a good passer," said Harrison, "just not a throw-it-forty-times-a-game type passer."

"We lost 23–14 to Oregon State at home," said Mildren, looking back nearly thirty-five years to his junior year as the Sooner quarterback. "It was a game we should not have lost. Collectively we didn't play very well. Bottom line was we weren't a very good football team at the time. We didn't have the ability to impose our will on a defense. To their everlasting credit, Fairbanks, Switzer, and Galen Hall made a decision to switch offenses in the middle of the season. We're talking about smart men and men with some courage, because the situation wasn't all peaches and cream. On the surface you can argue they made a pretty reckless decision. At the same time, they were putting their jobs on the line, because there was some grumbling."

Three weeks into the season, Oklahoma was 2–1 and had a week off before its annual fight with Texas in Dallas. The Longhorns were clearly the best team in the land at that moment, and while watching film of their vaunted wishbone attack, Oklahoma offensive coordinator Barry Switzer saw the tomorrow of Sooner football. Switzer had initially demurred when Fairbanks asked him to be offensive coordinator three years earlier, but eventually acquiesced, and, in doing so, forever changed for the better the future of Oklahoma football and the lives of hundreds of young men.

It was in his *Twelfth Night* that Shakespeare wrote: "But be not afraid of greatness: some are born great, some achieve greatness and some have greatness thrust upon 'em." Barry Switzer was a card-carrying member of the middle group. As a boy in the backwoods of Crossett, Arkansas, he lived in poverty. The family patriarch, Frank, was a bootlegger and serial philanderer who spent time in prison while his family lived in a shack on the outskirts of Crossett. A boyhood friend recalled that "among the kids at school there were no hard feelings toward Barry, but their parents viewed him as an outcast." When he was old enough to start dating, Barry Switzer hid in the backseat of the car, out of the view of the parents, while a friend went up and knocked on the door of the girl's home.

"Both of us spent most of our life running away from our background," said Switzer's younger brother Donnie years later. At a time when interracial friendships were rare, Barry Switzer became friends with some of the poor black families that lived near his own, and who often stopped by to buy cheap hooch from his father. In later years he became one of the first white college football coaches to genuinely appreciate black athletes as people rather than just football assets, and his ability to relate to kids from impoverished rural families made him the most successful recruiter of talent in college football history.

The wild life chosen by Barry's father, Frank Switzer, left his wife and Barry's mother, Mary Louise, a broken spirit. She insulated herself from the emotional abandonment with excessive drinking and prescription drugs, and disappeared inside the pages of novels, behavior her son Barry gave no truck. One night in August 1959, just as Switzer prepared to leave the family home and head back to school, Mary Louise attempted to engage her son in conversation. Switzer was annoyed that his mother was once again, as he put it, "loaded," and refused to talk to her, even turning away when she tried to kiss him good-bye. Just moments later, Mary Louise walked onto the porch of the shack and shot herself dead. "All she wanted was my love," Switzer later said. He never forgave himself for turning his face away from her kiss.

Frank Switzer outlived his wife for thirteen years before a car in which he was a passenger crashed and exploded in a fireball. His girlfriend was at the wheel of the car, and she was in a hurry to get him to the hospital because she had just shot him in the chest after catching him with another woman.

Determined to rise above what he was born to, Switzer, a star athlete in high school, enrolled at the University of Arkansas and set his sights on becoming a lawyer as a few of his uncles and cousins had done. At Arkansas he played football for teams coached by the wily Frank Broyles, and as the 1959 season approached, Switzer was looking forward to anchoring the offensive line from his position at center.

It was at the University of Arkansas that Barry Switzer met Jim Mackenzie, who, Switzer said, "had more influence on me in life than anyone I've ever met." After graduating in 1961, Switzer went to Aberdeen, Maryland, to fulfill a six-month military commitment. One day at Aberdeen "I heard my name called on the PA system," said Switzer. There was a phone call from his old line coach, Dixie White, who wanted to know if Switzer would return to Arkansas in the fall as a graduate assistant coach. "I never intended to be a coach," said Switzer, but the grad assistant job "beat going back to Little Rock and looking for a job. I thought I'd go back, live in the dorm, buy a new car, and use the part-time coaching to get me into law school."

Switzer soon gave up the dream of law school and instead became obsessed with coaching. Broyles's staff was widely considered the best in the country at the time, and as one of the bright young minds on it, Switzer was a prime target for poaching by coaches from other schools who visited Arkansas to learn the famed monster defense that had led the Razorbacks to prominence. Dartmouth came calling for Switzer, as did Virginia Tech and Tennessee, but Switzer spurned them all to stay alongside the father figure in his life, Mackenzie. When Oklahoma tapped Mackenzie for its top job, Switzer wanted to go with him. Broyles had a benevolent policy about helping assistants find head coaching jobs, but also had a rule that when they left they did so alone— there was no cherry-picking from the rest of the staff. Mackenzie wanted Switzer to come to Oklahoma with him, but it was up to Switzer to seek permission from Broyles.

On Christmas Day 1965, Switzer went to Broyles's home filled with the fear that accompanies asking an elder permission to do something that is known to be forbidden. Eyes on the floor, Switzer said simply, "I wanna go."

"You two make a good pair," said Broyles.

Five years later, Switzer was readying the Sooners' offensive plan for the Texas game when he had a realization. "Texas was the only team in the country running this offense," said Switzer, "and we had to defend against it. So when our defensive coaches studied the Texas offense they recognized our talent on offense was as good or better than Texas's at the offensive skill positions. We weren't very successful running the offense that we were running in 1970. It was my first experience as an offensive coordinator with the Houston veer. It was new to me, and I was in a learning process along with the team. And I knew our talent level was much better than our performance on the field. I wanted to give our players an opportunity to be successful. I thought the wishbone would be perfect for us.

"Before I could take my thoughts to Chuck Fairbanks to discuss them I had to have the assurance and agreement of the rest of the offensive staff," said Switzer. "They felt without a doubt that [an immediate switch to the wishbone] was what we should do. Then I needed the assurance of the defensive staff. We all met and agreed that we would present the idea to Chuck. So I, along with defensive coordinator Larry Lacewell, discussed it with Chuck. I discussed it first with Chuck, then Larry and I both did. We needed the support of the entire staff because they were an integral part of what was about to happen. It wasn't just an offensive decision. We couldn't have any second-guessing, and it was just as important to the defensive coaches because if it wasn't successful they were going to get their butts fired along with us."

"On our offense," said Fairbanks, "we had a whole bunch of speed guys like Greg Pruitt and Joe Wylie and Leon Crosswhite. We had lots of speed, and we had a quarterback, Jack Mildren, who had great running ability and great decision-making ability. And if we went to the wishbone, we could still take advantage of the time and the training that we had invested in executing the triple option, *and* switch from an offense that required passing ability to execute the run to a running offense that didn't depend on pro-style passing ability to make it work right."

Fairbanks listened to Switzer and Lacewell and said he'd think about the change. That night, at 3:30 A.M., Fairbanks telephoned his old coach and boss, Biggie Munn, in Michigan for counsel.

Roused from his bed, Munn listened as Fairbanks explained that he thought he wanted to change the Oklahoma offense over to the wishbone before the Texas game, just two weeks away. Munn told Fairbanks to call back at 9 A.M.

On the return call, Munn asked Fairbanks if he was convinced that this was the right thing to do.

Fairbanks said he was certain.

"Then don't look back," said Munn.

The Oklahoma coaching staff's method of informing the team was not a model of democracy in action. Jack Mildren said, "My reaction was normal, by which I mean, 'You *gotta* be kidding me.' On the other hand, my background was such growing up that I was a 'Yes sir' or 'No sir' kind of guy, and that was my response to the news. Part of me probably didn't want to believe it, but it was final. There was no discussion, there was no questioning. The coaches used words like 'We will' and 'We are.' I'm not even sure how much in-depth explanation was given about why we were making such a drastic change, and looking back it probably wasn't necessary to go into great detail about it."

When the date with Texas arrived, the Longhorns stuck it to the wishbone novices from Oklahoma, 41–9. It could have been viewed as a devastating loss, and no doubt was by some Sooner fans. Switzer saw something entirely different. "I knew we'd made the right decision," said Switzer, "even if it wasn't apparent on the floor of the Cotton Bowl when Texas thoroughly defeated us. But I left the Cotton Bowl knowing we were doing the right thing. And I could see the future. I could see down the road to where we were going and what we would be. Obviously the fans in the stands didn't recognize it. They thought we were on some muddy dirt road out lost in the wilderness, but I knew we were headed toward a superhighway."

"So we got beat in Texas with the wishbone," said Mildren, "and Switzer saw some silver lining in it, which was probably just him talking, but we got better and went to Boulder the next week and beat them [University of Colorado] when we probably shouldn't have, and we had some ups and downs the rest of the way, and some people were still clamoring for Chuck Fairbanks to be fired. That whole 1970 season was not my proudest moment. We never felt like we were in control, the coaching staff included, because none of them had coached the wishbone before, so they were learning on the fly just like us. I'm sure it took countless hours we weren't aware of on their part. But it ended up it was the right decision. How we started the season is not how we finished up. One thing Switzer and Galen [Hall] don't get credit for is their ability to teach what was expected of every one of us, player by player. In some respects they had to boil things down for us and then build up on that using Texas as a model."

It wasn't just the Oklahoma fans who weren't sure about the new course the coaching staff had set. Among the notable doubters was super-talented sophomore wide receiver Greg Pruitt. "I didn't like it at all," said Pruitt nearly thirty-five years later. "The reason I didn't like it was because I was a starting receiver. And when you go to the wishbone you lose one of those receivers. I went from starting receiver to second-team running back. The explanation to me was that I would get the ball more if they handed it to me in the wishbone. Since I wasn't going to start in the backfield, I couldn't figure out how I was going to get the ball more if I was standing on the sidelines.

"I was from Houston," continued Pruitt, "but my mom said I was too close to my friends and I had to leave Houston to go to college. My mom was kinda like the coaches. She said, 'Jump!' and I said 'How high?' I was so disappointed in the switch to the wishbone that I wanted to leave Oklahoma. Of course, Coach Fairbanks got wind of it. He asked me and I denied it. So I called my mom and told her I was going to quit Oklahoma and sit out a year and find another place to go. Usually, when you said something like that to my mom, she would scream at you. But she was very quiet—almost whispering—and she said, 'If that's what you want to do, then let me give you this telephone number.' "

"I just told you I'm going to quit and come home," said Pruitt to his mother. "Why are you giving me some random phone number? Whose number is this?"

Pruitt's mother said, "It's your uncle's phone number."

"Why would I want that?" said Pruitt.

"You need to call him because I didn't raise no quitters. You can stay with him."

"Now hold on a minute . . ."

"I'm telling you," said the mother, "if you quit, you can't come here. Just stay and do the best you can and things will work out."

"I stayed," said Pruitt, "and three weeks later, the guy starting in front of me, Everett Marshall, got hurt in the Iowa State game.

"I got a chance to play" and, said Pruitt, echoing Biggie Munn's advice to Fairbanks, "never looked back."

"I wasn't real happy when we switched offenses either," said Jon Harrison, "because I knew we weren't going to be throwing the ball as much. In the wishbone, you have a tight end, split end, and three guys in the backfield. I just knew the opportunity for me to contribute probably wasn't going to be pass catching, it would probably be with blocking. And that's really how I earned my job. They filmed and graded us every day at practice, and I really got my job not because I was the best athlete, but because I had the highest-percentage grades in blocking.

"Greg [Pruitt] was a split end and I was a flanker when we were in the veer," said Harrison. "When he went to running back, I went to the split. He wasn't too happy about it at first. I was afraid he was [going to transfer]. He talked about it. But it wasn't too long until he saw all the possibilities in the running game."

The Sooners won four of five games to close the regular season, losing only a 28–21 squeaker in Lincoln to the Cornhuskers. They took a 7–4 record to Houston to meet Alabama in the Astro-Bluebonnet Bowl, under the roof of the Astrodome, the world's first indoor sporting arena for sports traditionally played outdoors. Playing in front of his family and friends in his hometown, Greg Pruitt, running out of the wishbone, scored touchdowns on dashes of 58 and 25 yards. It wasn't until he was called back onto the field after the game to receive a trophy that he realized he'd been voted most outstanding offensive player in the 24–24 tie with the Tide. "I didn't know why they kept telling me I was needed on the field," said Pruitt. "I couldn't believe it."

COURTESY UNIVERSITY OF OKLAHOMA

In his first year as Oklahoma's head coach in 1966, Jim Mackenzie (left) brought together one of the finest young coaching staffs in history. Mackenzie died of a massive heart attack just a few months after the completion of his first season.

(Below) After the death of Mackenzie, Chuck Fairbanks (center, kneeling) was named head coach of the Sooners. Kneeling at the far left is Barry Switzer, chief proponent of the change to the wishbone offense. Second to Switzer's left is Galen Hall. First from the right kneeling is defensive line coach Jimmy Johnson. To his right, defensive coordinator Larry Lacewell.

COURTESY UNIVERSITY OF OKLAHOMA

COURTESY UNIVERSITY OF OKLAHOMA

After several lackluster seasons prior to 1971, Sooner fans were calling for the head of Chuck Fairbanks. Around Norman, a popular sign read: "Chuck Chuck."

Bob Devaney took over a Nebraska program that was believed to be beyond salvaging and turned it into Big Red.

LINCOLN JOURNAL STAR

LINCOLN JOURNAL STAR

LINCOLN JOURNAL STAR

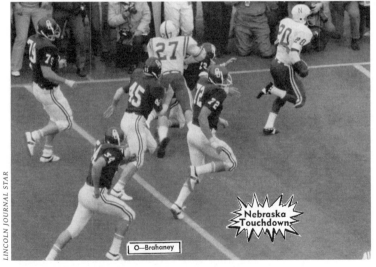

With the game scoreless early in the first quarter, Johnny Rodgers (20) fields a punt at his own 28-yard line while Sooner halfback Greg Pruitt (30) closes in for the tackle. Seconds later (second photo) Pruitt watches as Rodgers eludes other attempts to corner him before reversing course and heading for the sidelines. As Sooner split end Jon Harrison (12) closes in on Rodgers (third photo), he is blocked by Joe Blahak (27). The block, which many watching felt was illegal, sprung Rodgers for a touchdown.

Rodgers is greeted on the sidelines by Devaney after the punt return, one of the most memorable runs in college football history.

LINCOLN JOURNAL STAR

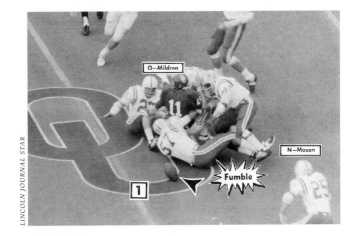

LINCOLN JOURNAL STAR

Nebraska's defensive scheme for the game moved hard-hitting Joe Blahak (27) from cornerback to safety to help stop the run. The switch paid off when Blahak delivered the blow to Jack Mildren (11) that caused this fumble. Monster back Dave Mason (25) recovered the ball while co-captain Jim Anderson (18) looked on. Nebraska scored on its ensuing possession.

LINCOLN JOURNAL STAR

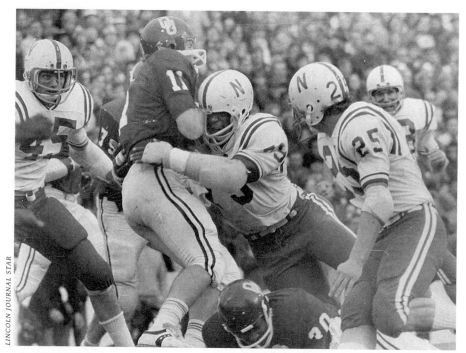

The Blackshirts shut down Oklahoma's outside running game, but Jack Mildren (11) successfully took the attack to the Husker middle. Here Mildren is stuffed by Rich Glover (79), who led Nebraska tacklers on the day.

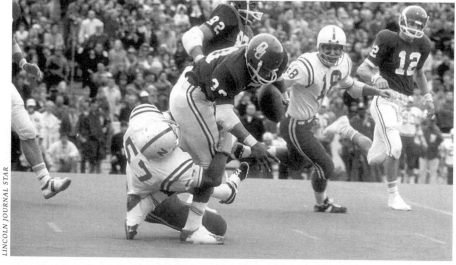

Greg Pruitt (30) was the most explosive running back in the country, but managed to get outside only once all day. To take up the slack, Mildren went to the air, hooking up on several key passes with Jon Harrison (12).

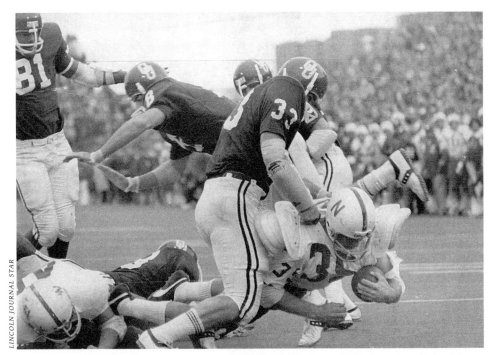

LINCOLN JOURNAL STAR

Jeff Kinney (35) punches in for a touchdown on Nebraska's bread-and-butter isolation play. It was the only game all season the Huskers wore tear-away jerseys. John Shelley (33) tries the impossible—that is to say, keeping Kinney out of the end zone.

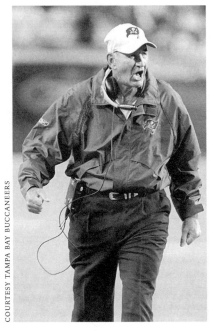

COURTESY TAMPA BAY BUCCANEERS

Monte Kiffin in 2003, as defensive coordinator of the Tampa Bay Buccaneers. Among the Nebraska defenders, he was a favorite. More than thirty years after the game, he still felt bad about stranding Bill Kosch on the corner against Jon Harrison.

COURTESY DALLAS COWBOYS

Jimmy Johnson coached the Oklahoma defensive line in 1971, and later led the University of Miami to the national championship and the Dallas Cowboys to two Super Bowl championships.

COURTESY DALLAS COWBOYS

Barry Switzer succeeded Fairbanks as Oklahoma's head coach and returned the Sooners to the top of the college game. As did Jimmy Johnson, he later coached the Dallas Cowboys to a Super Bowl title.

SIX

I returned and saw under the sun, that the race is not to the swift, nor the battle to the strong, neither yet bread to the wise, nor yet riches to men of understanding, nor yet favor to men of skill; but time and chance happeneth to them all.

—Ecclesiastes 9:11

THERE WAS JUST A SINGLE PLAY LEFT IN NEBRASKA'S 1970 regular season. It was late on the afternoon of November 21 in Lincoln, and the Cornhuskers were looking to run the table against their Big Eight opponents for the season. After dominating Wake Forest 36–12 to open their season, the Huskers had played the University of Southern California to a 21–21 tie. From that point forward, Nebraska had been perfect, defeating Army and Minnesota before systematically marching through its league schedule.

Now in the fading days of fall, Nebraska clung to a 28–21 lead over Oklahoma and the Sooners had the ball. There was time left for one more play. Jim Anderson was a junior cornerback for the Cornhuskers and, as had one of his secondary mates, Dave Mason, and quarterback Jerry Tagge, he had played his high school ball at Green Bay, Wisconsin's West High.

"Before that play started I realized it was an important play," said Anderson thirty-four years later. "I can remember vividly the couple of plays before it. On the play right before it, they had handed off to Joe Wylie on a counter. They had a long way to go but they ran a running play. He broke into the open field and was running wide open. He and I were on one half of the field all by ourselves and I tackled him, and I was really thrilled about that. On the last play of the game, we were playing for them to go for a touchdown, because they needed a touchdown to tie or to take a shot at winning the game. They threw it to Greg Pruitt and I saw it coming, so I took off as soon as Mildren threw the ball. It ended up being tipped up in the air, and I jumped over Pruitt and snatched it and came down with it in the end zone. I got up with the ball and ran with it a little bit and went out of bounds. I was so happy I threw the ball about fifty rows up into the stands. I wish I would have kept it."

Anderson's game-saving interception allowed Nebraska to finish its regular season 10–0–1, ranked third in both major national polls behind two undefeated and untied teams, Texas and Ohio State. The United Press International (UPI) poll was representative of the opinion of college football coaches, and was finalized after the regular season and before the bowl games were played. UPI voters had picked Texas as the national champion for 1970 long before the year-end holidays. The Associated Press (AP) poll was a sampling of the nation's sportswriters, and was not finalized until after all the major bowl games were played on New Year's Day. With ten wins under its belt, Nebraska headed to the Orange Bowl to play Louisiana State. The Orange Bowl, played under the lights in Miami, was traditionally the last game played in the college football season, preceded earlier in the day by the Cotton, Sugar, and Rose bowls.

In his thirty-seventh year of coaching, Bob Devaney knew from experience that time and chance happeneth to them all. On New Year's Day 1971, chance made a whirlwind tour of the country, starting in Dallas, traveling west to Pasadena, California, and then hurtling east like a lightning bolt to Miami.

Texas and its murderous wishbone, riding a thirty-game winning streak that dated to the third game of 1968, faced Notre

Dame in the Cotton Bowl for the second consecutive year. The 1970 Cotton Bowl had marked Notre Dame's first bowl appearance after a forty-five-year self-imposed ban on participating in postseason games. The Longhorns had surged from behind in 1970 to win 21–17 and solidify the 1969 national championship in both polls. As the two teams poised for battle on the first day of 1971, Texas was once again regarded as the best team in the country. The Irish had held the number one spot in the polls just weeks earlier with a 7–0 record, but dropped to number two after they struggled to a 10–7 win over Georgia Tech. The following week, at home in South Bend, Indiana, Notre Dame stumbled past Louisiana State, 3–0, and once again dipped in the polls. The Irish were ranked fourth before they closed out the season with a loss to Southern California, allowing Nebraska to slide into third place in the polls.

The 1971 Cotton Bowl was the most hotly anticipated bowl matchup of the day for numerous reasons. It was still a novelty to see Notre Dame in a bowl game, and the school's huge national following was anxious to see its excellent senior quarterback, Joe Theismann, attempt to avenge the loss to Texas the previous year. The first half of the game lived up to expectations. On Texas's first possession, quarterback Eddie Phillips motored 63 yards to the Notre Dame ten-yard line. There the Fighting Irish dug in their heels, and the Longhorns came away with three points when Happy Feller kicked a 23-yard field goal.

Theismann immediately drove Notre Dame the length of the field in ten plays, finishing off the series with a 26-yard touchdown pass. The Irish vaulted to a 21–3 lead until Phillips commanded an eighteen-play, 84-yard touchdown drive just before the half. Running back Jim Bertelsen hammered in from two yards, and Phillips threw to Danny Lester for the two-point conversion. Texas appeared to have gained some much-needed momentum, and over the course of the game the Longhorns outgained the Irish 426 yards to 359. They also outfumbled the Irish, coughing up the ball nine times and losing it six. Notre Dame won going away, 24–11.

With Texas knocked off, only Big Ten champs Ohio State and their mad general, Woody Hayes, had a chance to finish the year undefeated and untied. The 103,839 people packed into the Rose Bowl in Pasadena, and the Buckeye players, all knew that Texas had already lost. Ohio State was 9–0 on the season, and now only the Stanford Indians and their Heisman Trophy-winning quarterback, Jim Plunkett, stood between them and the Associated Press version of the national championship. Few observers seriously expected Stanford to put up much resistance, but the game was thrilling and hard fought.

On the very first play from scrimmage, Stanford flanker Eric Cross took the ball on a reverse and covered 41 yards before he was taken down at the Ohio State eighteen-yard line. Four plays later, Indian running back Jackie Brown scored a touchdown from four yards out. On its next possession, Stanford put together a minidrive of 32 yards that set up a field goal, and they led 10–0.

On the Ohio State sidelines, Woody Hayes was as apoplectic as only he could be. Hayes stormed up and down the bench igniting his charges. His defense stiffened, and the big eaters on the Buckeye offensive line moved 'em out. Twice before the half, All-American John Brockington punched the ball into the end zone. Order was restored on the field and the scoreboard as Ohio State took its 14–10 lead into the locker room. In the third quarter, the teams traded field goals, and then in living rooms all over the country football fans watched slack-jawed as Stanford proceeded to manhandle Ohio State for the duration of the game. The Indians won 27–17, and suddenly, all the way across the country in the Miami night, Nebraska's game against Louisiana State took on an entirely new sense of urgency for the Huskers. A victory meant the Huskers would be the only undefeated major college team in the country, and in all likelihood, the AP pick for national champions.

When Devaney's team had departed Lincoln for Miami there hadn't been much thought given to the notion that they might be playing for the right to be called the country's top team. "At that time we weren't really playing for the national championship," said

Joe Blahak, a sophomore defensive back on the team. "So many things had to fall in place for us. It wasn't until right before the game that we realized we could be national champions if we won."

"When we were at the stadium getting ready to play, they were still playing the Rose Bowl," said Jim Anderson, who had helped create the moment with his last-second interception six weeks earlier. "In fact, the start of our game was held up until that game was over. So, when we were running out of the tunnel onto the Orange Bowl turf, we had just found out were playing for the national championship. We didn't expect that, but all of a sudden it took on a whole new meaning. It was just happening all at once. You're ready to play and you just go out and play. During the game we weren't thinking about that [national championship], because once you're out there playing, you're just playing. Besides, that game against LSU was a real nail-biter."

Nebraska broke from the gate in a spirited dash for history. Paul Rogers put them on the board with a 25-yard field goal. Before the first quarter was over, senior Joe Orduna, who shared the tailback spot with junior Jeff Kinney, scored on a 3-yard touchdown run. Nebraska led 10–0. LSU kicked a field goal for the only score in the second quarter.

After another field goal early in the third quarter, LSU took control of the flow of the game. On the very last play of the quarter, LSU quarterback Buddy Lee chucked a 31-yard touchdown pass to Al Coffee. The conversion failed, but with one quarter left in the game, LSU led 12–10.

All year long, Devaney had platooned junior quarterbacks Van Brownson and Jerry Tagge, Jim Anderson's high school teammate back in Green Bay. With the brass ring in sight, Devaney handed the ball to Tagge, who now stepped behind center for the most important drive in Nebraska football history up to that point. Working the clock and the LSU defense for slightly more than nine minutes, Tagge guided the Huskers 66 yards to the LSU one-yard line. With 6:10 showing on the clock, Tagge kept the ball himself and bulldozed into the end zone.

LSU substituted future Baltimore Colts star Bert Jones for Buddy Lee, and Jones began to move the Tigers toward victory. With just forty-five seconds left in the game, Nebraska linebacker Bob Terrio, a junior college transfer who had arrived at Nebraska hoping to be a running back, intercepted a Jones pass.

In the warmth of a holiday evening in Florida, only Bob Devaney knew how far Bob Devaney had come from the day he started as coach at Big Beaver High in Michigan, following a coach with an 0–40 record. The quarterback on his first team "was terrible, but he was a good thinker," said Devaney. "He started all the games. He was the superintendent's son. In one game we had twelve men on the field and the kid noticed it. In the huddle he called a sweep toward our bench and told the dumbhead to drop onto our sidelines and maybe the referees wouldn't notice. On the next play we ended up with seven men on the field.

"It wasn't bad at Big Beaver," said Devaney, "it was terrible. We had only one good back in the time I was there. He was a fullback who stood six feet five and weighed one-nineteen. He was the only one who could squeeze through the holes our line made. We had another back who was a triple threat—he threatened to quit three times."

As the seconds ticked away in the Orange Bowl, Devaney must have felt his team would get the nod as national champions from the sportswriters who voted in the AP poll, but he couldn't be certain. Already, Notre Dame coach Ara Parseghian was stumping for his team to be tapped as number one. The Irish had beaten Texas, Parseghian said, and in doing so had "accepted the greater challenge" than Nebraska.

Devaney chose not to stand by and let Parseghian besmirch the accomplishments of the Cornhuskers. "Not even the pope could vote for Notre Dame as number one," said Devaney. Parseghian said Devaney's remark was of questionable taste, but Devaney said "I was afraid Ara's comments might influence the vote."

When the writers' votes were all counted, Nebraska was number one. "The writers were too smart to take some coach's word," said Devaney. "Coaches don't know anything about rankings."

Just in case there was any doubt about the final vote, two weeks later, on January 14, 1971, President Richard Nixon visited Lincoln and proclaimed the Cornhuskers national champions. Senior captains Jerry Murtaugh and Dan Schneiss joined Devaney alongside Nixon as the 8,000 people stuffed into the Nebraska field house shrieked their approval.

At long last, and for the first time ever, Big Red was number one.

The championship season of 1970 was the first in which Nebraska sophomore flanker Johnny Rodgers was eligible for varsity competition. Anyone in Nebraska who knew football—and that was most people—knew that Johnny Rodgers was a high school All-American at Omaha Tech, located in the state's largest city, hard by the eastern border with Iowa. In his first year playing for Big Red, Rodgers was a major force. He caught thirty-nine passes for 710 yards, scored eleven touchdowns, and was the team's leading kickoff and punt returner.

Johnny Rodgers was born talented. To see him in action on a football field was to see the purest possible type of athleticism. When he ran with the ball it seemed as though a tornado was loose on the field. The top of his body went one way, his hips another, and his feet and legs still another. Defenders were left grasping at air and shaking their heads. No one who saw Johnny Rodgers run, even if it was just on television, ever forgot the sight. In addition to the shake-and-bake runs, Rodgers was a superb possession receiver who caught any ball he could get his hands on.

As gifted as he was, Rodgers was also a perfect example of the inflated sense of entitlement that often affects athletes who are incapable of placing their skills in the context of real life. Rodgers had a jock mentality to the extreme, and believed that so long as he could run fast and score touchdowns people were required to wink at his shortcomings off the field, no matter how egregious those shortcomings were. In Rodgers's case, his off-field antics spanned the spectrum of irresponsibility. By the time he was sixteen years old, Rodgers had fathered two children, the first when he was fourteen. By the time he left Nebraska lugging the Heisman Trophy in 1972, Rodgers had fathered two additional children.

As summer approached in 1971, however, it became clear that Rodgers's reckless behavior wasn't limited strictly to the morally questionable. On Thursday, May 20, Rodgers appeared in Lancaster District Court and pleaded guilty to a felony charge of larceny from a person, based on his involvement in the armed robbery of a gas station in Lincoln exactly one year earlier.

The summary of the case appeared in the *Lincoln Journal Star* on Friday, May 21, 1971.

Felonies

(Maximum penalty of imprisonment in the
Nebraska Penal Complex)

Johnny S. Rodgers, 19, of 1005 Harper Hall, charged with taking property of value from the person of Glen Griggs, May 20, 1970, without the consent of Griggs and without putting the said Griggs in fear by threats or by the use of force or violence, waived preliminary hearing, bound over to District Court, $5,000 bond.

Judge William Hastings told Rodgers he had the right to a jury trial, but Rodgers waived that right and entered his guilty plea immediately. Hastings reduced the bond to $2,000 at the request of Rodgers's attorney, and Cornhusker assistant coach Tom Osborne posted the bond for Rodgers's release.

Exactly what transpired at the Derby Oil service station at Ninth and South in Lincoln, at approximately 3:15 A.M. on the night of May 20, 1970, is unclear. It is inconceivable, however, that "said Griggs" was not "in fear." According to police reports and court filings, two men entered the station, pulled a handgun on Griggs, and took $91.50 from the till, while a third man waited outside with what appeared to be a rifle. According to Lancaster County Attorney Paul Douglas at the time, the investigation of the robbery revealed that Rodgers was the individual holding the pistol when he and Randy McCall, another Nebraska student, took the money from Griggs. The third man, James Glass, of Omaha, waited outside. Other reports indicated that Rodgers was the man outside the station, allegedly with the rifle, while Glass and McCall grabbed the money.

All three men involved were slapped with the same charge, and all eventually received the same sentence: two years probation. It was a plea deal, pure and simple. At the time, Paul Douglas told a reporter that he was being criticized for the way he handled the case—i.e., there was a perception in some quarters that Rodgers was being handled gently because of his status as a Husker star.

More than thirty years after the fact, Douglas, the former prosecutor, insisted that the plea deal was not only justified but was the only option open to the authorities. The case—which was only solved when one of Rodgers's accomplices, under pressure from his girlfriend, sought out police and confessed—occurred against a backdrop of racial strife. In fact, it happened on a night of racial unrest in Lincoln, and prosecutors were loath to risk sparking any further unrest by targeting a local minority hero such as Rodgers, who was not only a well-known personality in town but had no significant prior criminal record.

What's more, the prosecution's case wasn't particularly sound, Douglas admitted. The facts of the case were hazy, and prosecutors, who were relying almost exclusively on the testimony of a coconspirator, could not establish with any certainty the identity of the gunman inside the store. Although at the time Douglas told reporters that he believed Rodgers had been more than just a lookout, nearly thirty-five years later he conceded that he may have been mistaken. "I don't know if I was in error back then or not," said Douglas. "You know, it's been a long time. I remember the incident because it involved Johnny Rodgers, and I have the impression that he was in the car on the outside, but that may not be true."

In the end, Douglas acknowledged, given the lack of clear evidence and the racial turmoil the case could have ignited, the prosecution simply chose to make a deal and make the whole thing go away.

After his plea, but before sentencing, Rodgers said, "I've had plenty of time to think [about] why I did it—one year to think about why I did it—but I still don't know why I did it. It was just stupidity." Rodgers claimed he considered giving the money back, but he didn't, and he wasn't the one who initially stepped forward and confessed. His performance on the field for the entire season following the robbery certainly wasn't hindered by any secret guilt. Prior to receiving the probation sentence, Rodgers's primary concern seemed to be whether or not he could continue to play football. "I can't make any definite plans until after the trial [sic]," said Rodgers, who no longer faced the prospect of a trial. "Of course, I plan to keep playing football if I can. And I intend to work this summer at Midwest Supply in Omaha and work with the Bryant Basketball Center." Asked if he noticed any change in the disposition of the people around him, Rodgers said, "The majority of the people have tried to help, but some have bothered me."

On Friday, June 25, 1971, Rodgers received the sentence of two years probation. His attorney, Dave Pierson, urged Judge Hastings to grant probation so that Rodgers could "continue to mature and develop as a citizen" and said that the events in the courtroom would have a "substantial impact on the young man's future." The judge noted that several individuals affiliated with the Boys' Clubs in Omaha had spoken on Rodgers's behalf. "Perhaps the real tragedy," said Hastings, addressing Rodgers, "is the effect of your acts on the children in the Boys' Clubs who looked up to you." Furthermore, Hastings reminded him, only Rodgers himself could determine "what you're going to do and how you're going to conduct yourself." With a final warning from the judge that if Rodgers violated the terms of probation he would be hauled back into court on the felony charge (which carried a possible sentence of not less than one or more than seven years in the Nebraska Penal Complex), the Cornhusker star was off the hook.

Bob Devaney, however, still had to decide whether to allow Rodgers to play for him during the 1971 season. As a coach who had just won a national championship, Devaney held nearly unlimited sway over public opinion in Nebraska. After winning the title, Devaney, also the athletic director at the university, had gone before Nebraska's unicameral state legislature and asked for a tax on cigarettes to raise money for a new indoor sports arena at the school. The tax was swiftly put in place. Eventually, said Boyd Epley, people came to believe that Bob Devaney could make the rain stop simply by setting foot on the practice field. "He'd come into the weight room to get out of the rain," said Epley. "And he'd keep looking out the window until finally he'd say, 'Well, looks like it's gonna clear up.' Then he'd go back out onto the practice field and the rain would stop. The legend evolved because it happened many, many times, but he was just looking out the window like anyone else would do."

Whatever Devaney decided regarding Rodgers, it would be viewed as the proper decision. If he booted Rodgers from the team, it would be seen as a necessary disciplinary measure. If he allowed Rodgers to play, it would be an act of benevolence. Privately, Devaney acknowledged the whole situation would have been a hell of a lot simpler if Rodgers wasn't such a good player. If Rodgers were a scrub, no one would care if he were given a second chance. The gravity of Devaney's eventual decision was lessened when the university's student tribunal and the dean of student development permitted Rodgers to stay in school on probationary status. On Tuesday, July 6, with the football season and the defense of the national championship on the horizon, Devaney announced his decision. "We do not condone John's actions in any way," said Devaney. "But we also feel that to deprive him of the opportunity to play football would work against the aims of the probation already established." After careful deliberation by the entire coaching staff, Devaney said, they all agreed to follow the course set by the court and the university.

Rodgers, who turned twenty the previous day, said the decision was "a great birthday present. I wanted to play football more than anything. There is not even the slim chance I'll ever get into any more trouble of any kind."

In later years, Devaney said of Rodgers that "John had a knack for being in the wrong place at the wrong time, except when he had a football in his hands." That Rodgers needed a firm guiding hand was clear, and Devaney asked Tom Osborne, who had posted bail for Rodgers, to step into that role. Osborne was so serene and quiet that his friends in high school had called him Yak. When he had joined Devaney's staff in 1962, Osborne was viewed as a bit of a square by the other coaches (including Devaney), who spent their off time hanging out in bars and playing golf. Gradually, however, Devaney and everyone else at Nebraska realized that Osborne possessed a surplus of character and quiet resolve. Perhaps the hope was that it would rub off on Rodgers. If it were going to, it would rub off at 6 A.M. "John hated two things," said Devaney: "running, and getting up early."

Rodgers and Osborne ran together every morning. "We talked and we ran, we ran and we talked," said Rodgers years later. Rodgers wasn't the first or last star athlete who required babysitting, but he was lucky to have someone as sincere as Tom Osborne fall from the sky as his babysitter.

In their spring practices during 1971, the Oklahoma backfield of Jack Mildren, Leon Crosswhite, Joe Wylie, and Greg Pruitt grew more and more familiar with the wishbone. They were helped along by Barry Switzer, who grasped the nuances of the attack more firmly with each passing day. Once the 1970 season had ended, Switzer received some firsthand tutoring from the origina- tor of the scheme at Texas, Emory Bellard.

"Lots of college and high school coaches from all over the country were either coming to our campus to learn about the wishbone or calling us constantly in those days," said Bellard. One day in early 1971, one of the phone calls was from Chuck Fairbanks. "Being from Oklahoma, Darrell [Royal] had a pretty good relationship with Chuck," said Bellard. "Darrell came into my office and said, 'Barry Switzer will be calling you. I want you to tell him about the wishbone.' I talked to Switzer time and time again. He got everything on a direct line from me. After a while, I said, 'Darrell, are you sure we should be telling them so much?' But that tells you a lot about the character of Darrell Royal."

In later years, Royal laughed and said, "Looking back, maybe we were a little too generous. Yeah, they [Oklahoma] became prolific, but did they ever win thirty in a row with it?"

With the imparted wisdom of Bellard and his own relentless approach to learning, Barry Switzer was certain that 1971 would prove that he and the Oklahoma staff had been dead right when they switched offenses in 1970. As the time for summer practices that led up to the first game of 1971 neared, Switzer could hardly contain his enthusiasm. "We've tried to go through every defensive structure and technique we might face," said Switzer. "We've tried to go through all things that could occur. We tried to come up with a formula to have the understanding so we could physically execute the offense. Now we think we've got what we want. It's all in a package—a complete understanding."

During a preseason golf outing with the local press, it was obvious Switzer's mind was elsewhere. As soon as he holed out on the eighteenth green, Switzer hurried back to the office to work on the offense.

"I'm really enthused," Switzer confided later that night to local newspaper columnist Bob Hurt. "I know that we know what to do to get the job done."

SEVEN

There's a new foot on the floor, my friend,
And a new face at the door, my friend,
A new face at the door.

—Alfred, Lord Tennyson, "The Death of the Old Year"

The calendar read 1971, but the 1960s were still sputtering toward their conclusion in the summer before college football's game of the century. In June, the Supreme Court overruled attempts by the federal government to stop publication by the *Washington Post* and the *New York Times* of a secret report on the war in Vietnam. The report came to be known as the Pentagon Papers. In the same session two days earlier, the court cleared Muhammad Ali of charges stemming from his refusal to be inducted into the U.S. Army four years earlier, when his name was Cassius Clay.

The space race between the United States and Russia, a long-running battle of one-upsmanship, had begun petering out the instant American astronauts set foot on the moon in July 1969. By July 1971, no one seemed to notice or care much that astronauts were driving around on the lunar surface in a high-tech dune buggy, or that a few weeks earlier after a seemingly successful reentry, three Russian cosmonauts who had set the record for the most orbits of earth were found dead in their Soyuz spacecraft at its landing site in Kazakhstan.

For more than ten years the American military presence in

Vietnam, and the nearly 46,000 American deaths it had caused, hung like a millstone around the country's neck. In July 1971, many of the nation's young men were still fighting and dying in Southeast Asia for reasons few people could comprehend, but some positive trends were emerging. The military tipped its cap to the peace movement by changing the words screamed by soldiers during bayonet training from "Kill! Kill!" to "Yah! Yah!" There was promising news in July when eleven combat deaths were reported for the month. That was the lowest KIA total since 1965, and was a stark contrast to the three hundred KIA averaged per month during the fiercest fighting. In early August, news leaked out of Stockholm that North Vietnam and the United States had arranged for the secret release of 183 American POWs who would be transported to New York on a chartered SAS airliner.

Signs of a slightly less grim national mood continued into the autumn of 1971. Disney World opened in Orlando, Florida, in early October at a cost of $400 million. Local residents and officials in Orlando were nervous about Disney World and the ten million visitors it was expected to attract in its first year of operation. The theme park created 7,000 new jobs during weak economic times, and gave people reason to smile. Disneyland in California had a talking likeness of Abraham Lincoln, but Disney World had automated versions of all thirty-seven presidents. A visiting writer from the *Los Angeles Times* wrote that "Disneyland is a trial balloon. Disney World is a trip to the moon . . . only Disney can build the perfect city-state out of a hunk of ugly land whose only previous purpose seemed to be holding a chunk of the world together. Disney World hasn't any clutter and it's an ecological dream. Clean. Orderly. Enticing."

Americans were clearly in the mood to smile. By the middle of October, more than 20 million happy-face buttons had been sold. The yellow buttons had two black eyes and a permanent blank smile. The smiley face had no nose, but you could buy it on everything from T-shirts to toilet seats to made-to-order items at Cartier, the famed jeweler, in New York. A single general store in Lakewood, California, sold 30,000 smiley-face buttons in just four months. The nation was quite literally letting its hair down: At the University of Arizona, Michael Prost, a twenty-five-year-old man with shoulder-length hair, beat out five women for the school's homecoming-queen nomination. In Enid, a town in north central Oklahoma, high school students staged a protest against hair-length restrictions in the dress code. The pursuit of the hirsute life was not solely the purview of America's youth. A Soviet state-published magazine was disturbed by all the hair it saw in its midst and reported that "long hair and other extremes of fashion are unnatural and unhealthy" and that long hair on a man was a "sign of failure and inferiority." One could almost see veterans of the battle of Stalingrad slowly shaking their heads from side to side in agreement with older Americans. "It could be worse," went a joke making the rounds in America: "You could be the barber in a college town."

Kim Casali, a New Zealander, created an inescapable fad—the "love is . . ." cartoons, inspired by love notes she made for her future husband. She signed the drawings of round-faced little people with a simple, loopy *kim*, using a tiny circle to dot the "i." Each panel began with the words "love is . . ." and was followed by a sentiment such as "never having to say you're sorry" or "putting a rose in her room while she's convalescing." Love, it seemed, could conquer all, even the Iron Curtain. At least it did in the case of Elizabeth Newmann, an East German woman who was arrested by police in 1969 along with Lyle Jenkins, a fellow from Norfolk, Virginia. The two were in love, and Jenkins was charged with trying to entice Ms. Newmann to the West, while she was charged with deserting her country and was forced to say goodbye to Jenkins when he was booted to the other side of the curtain. But Jenkins persevered and started a "Free Elizabeth" campaign that eventually became a public relations nuisance for the East Germans. Elizabeth was freed on October 27, 1971, and allowed to go to the U.S. so she could marry Jenkins.

In the world of sports, there was some love lost when the New York Giants football team announced that as of 1974 it would play its home games in New Jersey. New York football fans felt like Woodstock attempting to kick the football in a famous *Peanuts* comic strip at the time. The ball wobbled slowly, then fell on top of the bird, crushing him. In St. Louis, Joe Torre led the National League in hitting on his way to being named league MVP. (On Thanksgiving Day, Torre would attend the Nebraska vs. Oklahoma game in Norman.) It was the Pittsburgh Pirates, however, behind the bats of Roberto Clemente, Manny Sanguillen, Willie Stargell, and Dave Cash—all hitting better than .300—who won the World Series over Baltimore in October. In Boston, Bobby Orr signed a five-year contract believed to be the largest in sports history at the time, but both the Bruins and their golden boy were mum on the amount the two-time NHL most valuable player would be paid.

In Washington, a House subcommittee was listening to testimony regarding the injuries of today caused by the playing surface of tomorrow—Astroturf. The synthetic grass was first used in the Houston Astrodome in 1966 by baseball's Astros and the American Football League's Oilers. In 1967, Indiana State became the first college to install an Astroturf field. Soon, nearly every football field in America was covered with either Astroturf or one of a multitude of knockoffs with names such as Tartan Turf, Gras, Stadia Turf, All-Pro, DurraTurf, Lectron, and Kureha. Experts in sports medicine and football were trotted before the committee, and Ed Garvey, the executive director of the NFL Players Association, called on NFL team owners to stop installing the fake surfaces until more safety studies were done. In perhaps the least enlightening and most amusing sports-related testimony since Casey Stengel appeared on the Hill in 1958 to testify before the Senate Anti-Trust and Monopoly Sub-Committee hearing chaired by Senator Estes Kefauver, Washington Redskin John Wilbur said the artificial grass was no good because "it makes defensive linemen quicker and I'm an offensive lineman."

Everyday life in Nebraska and Oklahoma reflected the changing times, albeit on a smaller scale. One "love is . . ." cartoon not drawn by Kim Casali was on a banner hanging outside the house at 1408 Dorcas Street in Omaha: ". . . welcoming him home from Vietnam!!" was the completion of the verse written by Mrs. Alfred Miller, who sat on her porch all day on Tuesday, August 31, waiting for her man, Sergeant Al Miller, to arrive home. During a year in Vietnam as a helicopter gunner, Al Miller, a 1966 graduate of South High in Omaha, had survived two air crashes without a serious injury. Miller's homecoming was storybook compared to the alternative. Earlier in August, Margie Scott received word that her husband, Sergeant Donald E. Scott of rural Collinsville, just outside of Tulsa, had been killed in action. He was the 1,075th Oklahoman killed in Vietnam.

A group of Oklahomans who fought closer to home, the state's law officers, were in desperate need of a pay increase. The average monthly salary for sheriffs' deputies in Oklahoma was $452.09, while their bosses, the sheriffs, made $582.50 per month. The sheriffs' pay was guaranteed by state law, but that was not the case for deputies, whose pay varied wildly. In Bryan County, down near the Texas border, some officers were upset when they received a $10-per-month raise because it put their income above the official poverty level and made them ineligible for food welfare.

At a bank in Oklahoma City, a stunningly beautiful lady named Sharon Wallace was hired as the first-ever woman bank guard in town, but faced her own unique problems regarding respect. She was trained in karate, she said, but was not permitted to carry a gun. "It is customary that a lady guard does not wear a gun," said Wallace's boss, E. Paul Weekley. "The routine gun and holder do not look good on a woman. She's good to have around if women get sick or faint and need to be taken into the ladies lounge." Wallace's problems paled in comparison to local strippers Rita Hodges, Sharon Dennis, and Sheryl Fitzpatrick, who announced they intended to sue the city over an antitopless ordinance that was cutting into their earnings at the Guys and Dolls Lounge on Farnam Street.

In Sapulpa, south of Tulsa, a junior high teacher faced a school board hearing on charges of "willful neglect of duty and cruelty" over an incident when he paddled thirty students. At another school in Washington County, near the Kansas border, school officials refused to allow a thirteen-year-old girl to attend class because she was wearing pants. The now-antiquated world of football and sock hops was facing a new decade.

High school students in Nebraska revealed that Big Red's number one ranking at the end of the 1970 season wasn't any reason for them to stay close to home when it came time for college. Carol Herzog, of Bloomfield, a small town near the South Dakota border, said Nebraska "has to become number one in more than just football before I decide to stay." Her feelings were echoed by Gary Nicholas, of North Platte, who said he saw "no future here" and hoped to attend the University of Colorado, "where you feel like you are with the world instead of being out in the sticks." If that was the view from the inside looking out by some young people in the Midwest, most citizens saw more water in the glass. After all, it was almost football season.

On Monday, August 9, 1971, the head coaches of the Big Eight's varsity football squads joined roughly a thousand other diners who hung on their every word at the conference's annual kickoff luncheon in Kansas City, Missouri. The crowd was largely made up of Missouri fans, and Mizzou coach Al Onofrio said, "I can't believe the optimism of all these other coaches. Devaney has a unique problem in having three quarterbacks this year. Last year he won the national championship with two [Tagge and Van Brownson]. Just so he'll have something to shoot at, he's going to try it with three this year." Onofrio was alluding to highly touted Husker sophomore Dave Humm.

Colorado's Eddie Crowder, who played his college ball at Oklahoma, said "it was nice to be back at the University of Missouri quarterback luncheon. The emcee suggested I tell you who I think we can beat this year. I think we can beat Redlands and Claremont Normal. Unfortunately, we're not playing them." Kansas State's Vince Gibson followed. "Personally," said Gibson, "I think we're all gonna be seeing a lot of red this year. The only thing I hate about Nebraska is that they don't have any road games. When they play on the road, so many of their fans follow them it's like a home game for them."

Fairbanks and Devaney were next on the speaking list, and Gibson told the crowd, "You'll notice how we're all a heck of a lot cockier talking before Devaney and Fairbanks than we would be after."

When Fairbanks stepped up to the microphone, he was quick to acknowledge that Oklahoma fans had big expectations for the coming season. After one spring practice, Fairbanks said, a fan walked up to him and said the Sooners looked really good. "I asked him if he'd been up to see Nebraska practice or down to see Texas or out to see Southern California," said Fairbanks. "It seems like about ten years ago Bud Wilkinson was feeling good and managed to get all three of them scheduled for the same season."

"Well," said Devaney with his trademark impish grin, "we're all gonna be good again this year—today at least." Even though Devaney was smiling, the Big Eight was, in fact, a conference loaded with talent both on the field and on the sidelines. Iowa State's head coach, Johnny Majors, would lead the University of Pittsburgh to a national championship five years off in the future. Crowder, from Colorado, had a team loaded with dynamite players, including a world-class sprinter named Cliff Branch, who later became a standout receiver on multiple Super Bowl–winning teams for the Oakland Raiders. And every game against Missouri was a bloodletting. "You knew when you went to play Missouri," said Oklahoma offensive lineman Dean Unruh, "that their defense was going to hit you in the mouth." (It should be noted here that when a football player says "hit you in the mouth" it's an allusion to the toughness of an opponent, not dirty play.)

There was little question that Oklahoma and Colorado faced the most daunting nonconference foes. The opening stretch of the season for the Sooners included Southern Methodist, Pittsburgh, Southern California, and Texas before they started conference play against Colorado. Before meeting the Sooners, the Buffaloes had dates at Ohio State and Louisiana State. By contrast, Nebraska opened the season against a talented Oregon team, but after that didn't face anything like the firing-squad competition Oklahoma would see. "Can't figure how we missed scheduling Russia," said Oklahoma defensive coordinator Larry Lacewell.

Before summer practice began, the Sooners had a team picnic on Friday, August 20. The next day, players endured physical exams and then hustled out to Owen Field to engage in a ritual as old as football and cameras: press day. Ninety Sooner players spent the day in ridiculously contrived poses for representatives from eight television stations, fifteen radio stations, and a dozen newspapers. Defensive linemen pretended to leap on fumbles and the shutters clicked as the players flew through the air. Running backs faked high-knee poses and stiff-armed imaginary defenders and the exposures were fired off. For the rest of the season, when the player was mentioned in type, this was the hokey image the public saw of him. Asked how picture day was going, Fairbanks said, "I'll have to look at the film first." On a more serious note, Fairbanks said the team "looks to be in better physical condition than any team we've had at this point."

The season had barely passed the picture-taking phase when word hit the papers on August 22 that seats on the bus caravan to Dallas for the game with Texas on October 9 were filling up quick. The cost was $12.50 for the round-trip, ticket to the game not included.

When practice started on August 23, Fairbanks had a surprise in store for his players. NCAA rules mandated the first three days of fall practice be devoid of contact, and helmets were the only equipment worn. Two practices a day—two-a-days, as football people called them—was the standard for football teams early in training camp. Fairbanks decided that on the three helmet-only days that opened camp, socks-and-jocks days, he would schedule three shorter workouts rather than two longer ones. The shorter workouts would help the players maintain their focus on what were primarily learning days for them and teaching days for the coaches. This was the kind of decision Fairbanks was known for by his players. "Fairbanks was sort of like a general, and he didn't get real involved with stuff," said wide receiver Jon Harrison. "He was up in the tower, and the assistants ran practice. He didn't say much of anything during practice. He was a CEO type of guy who let his staff do their jobs."

"Good zip! We're getting something down out here!" Fairbanks said to no one in particular as the Sooners buzzed through three days of three-a-days in socks and jocks. After practice, Fairbanks said the schedule was working out well. "We set it up this way to keep the players mentally fresh, and it worked." The total on-field time for each day of three-a-days was four hours and fifteen minutes, or twenty minutes fewer than the two-a-day total of previous seasons.

The emphasis before the hitting started was on teaching, timing, and cohesiveness as a unit. Achieving those things required repetition, particularly among the four backs who would work the wishbone attack: Jack Mildren, Leon Crosswhite, Joe Wylie, and Greg Pruitt. "I don't know if I buy that you had to be smart to play quarterback in the wishbone," said Mildren years later. "You needed people who understood repetition. Leon had to run the same path over and over again, for instance, but back in Norman in those days, we had a practice field that helped us remember. It was a grass practice field with a bit of Astroturf with path lines painted on it, so it was kind of like a golf-swing training exercise, if you will. So, I followed the same path on every practice rep, and Leon did and Joe did and Greg did. Theoretically, the repetition would make us all stay in synch."

Under the watchful eye of Barry Switzer, the Sooner backfield jelled more and more. "Coach Fairbanks was a great coach," said Greg Pruitt. "I think if you look at the whole staff, a lot of those guys went on to become great coaches. So he was very smart in picking coaches to make his job easier. He was more a disciplinarian. He was a guy that you didn't like very much at the time, but being an older guy now, I understand. Bad guy, good guy, they had to play that. Someone had to be close enough to you to understand what the problem really was, and someone had to be stern enough that you feared him enough that you didn't do something that would get the whole program in trouble. Switzer was a genius as a coach. He had an aura about him, and players were very comfortable around Coach Switzer. At that time, coaches always kept their distance from players. They only allowed themselves a certain amount of closeness because when they had to make a tough decision they didn't want personal feelings to get in the way. Switzer was different. He would talk with you, laugh with you, joke with you, whatever—but when it came time to work, you *worked*. And the guy that worked the most and performed the best got the job. He was a great communicator and motivator. He knew all the tricks."

"The reason you run a play a thousand times in practice is because nine-hundred and ninety-nine isn't enough," said Switzer, explaining the execution of the wishbone with passion in his voice more than thirty years removed from his days as an assistant at Oklahoma. "The quarterback has rules of execution he's taught from spring practice, two-a-days, game preparation, and film meetings. He has a tremendous knowledge of defensive structures. He recognizes defensive fronts, he knows how we attack them, he knows the blocking scheme of our offensive line, and he understands the vulnerability of the defense. He has a great working knowledge of what might happen before the ball is snapped and an idea of how he'll respond. And that's why you practice, so in the game it comes as near to automatic as possible.

"There are predetermined plays called in the huddle," said

Switzer. "That's not left up to the quarterback other than the execution of the play. When we talk about running the wishbone, the basic concept of the alignment is to run a triple option: The first option is the quarterback hands it to the fullback on a slant dive between the guard-tackle gap. Whether the quarterback goes with the first option is decided in part by a predetermined read of how the defense is lined up when the quarterback goes to the line of scrimmage. So, in some cases, he'll know before the ball is snapped whether he's going to give it to the fullback. If the defense is lined up in a formation that does not dictate a presnap read, then the quarterback doesn't know until after the ball is snapped whether he's going to give the ball to the fullback or keep it. Once the play is in motion, there are two read keys for the quarterback—the inside read key and the outside read key. The inside key read comes first, and it varies from play to play. The quarterback must execute against what he sees in the defense's reaction to the play. If the inside defensive key does not respond to the possibility that the ball still may be given to the first option—if the defender doesn't play it in a particular way—then the ball is given to the fullback.

"If the inside key reacts to take away the first option," said Switzer, "the quarterback takes the ball and executes the second option. The second option determines whether the quarterback keeps the ball or pitches the football, based on the outside key. If the outside key responds a certain way, he keeps the football. If the outside key responds by moving to tackle the quarterback, the football is pitched to the pitch man. In the wishbone offense, the outside option has a lead blocker for either the quarterback or the pitch back, depending on the blocking scheme call.

"So," continued Switzer, "if the quarterback keeps the ball, he'll have an inside blocker against the defender who's assigned to the quarterback. And if the ball is pitched to the halfback, he'll have a man to block the defender designed to take the pitch back. That's why the three-back offense was very difficult to stop. Big plays are made on the perimeter of defenses, and in the wishbone the perimeter of the defense is attacked with a runner with a lead blocker. A lot of big plays happened at the corners."

The man who would make the wishbone go was Jack Mildren, and his coaches and teammates had complete confidence in him. "You're talking about a rare person and special athlete in Jack Mildren," said Fairbanks. "Every coach should be fortunate enough sometime in his life to coach somebody like that. I was so lucky to have somebody so gifted and such a solid, true-blue young man. He's just special. I can't say any more about him."

"Jack Mildren was the best quarterback we ever had at Oklahoma," said Greg Pruitt. "The ball was always where it was supposed to be. Whether it was with the fullback, or he kept it or pitched it. If you watched film of all the other wishbone quarterbacks at places like Texas and Alabama, they faked it to the fullback, came out and if the defense ran past them, they kept the ball. But if the defense checked the quarterback, he'd never challenge that defensive player, he just pitched the ball, so the defender could go from him to the pitch man. That's what every wishbone quarterback did, except Jack. Jack challenged the defender, and always made the last guy hesitate because he would always face him and threaten him. And once the defender hesitated, it was a touchdown in many cases. All we needed was that half step. Make him commit. You didn't see that in other option quarterbacks. He was a tough, physical player. If he turned upfield with the ball— and you see this a lot, the quarterback turns it up and the pitch back stops running—Jack would jump all over you if you didn't follow him down the field. He still wanted to pitch the ball ten or fifteen yards down the field sometimes."

When Darrell Royal said the wishbone required a quarterback who wasn't always running out of bounds to avoid getting hit, he may have had Mildren in mind. He was just 6' and 199 pounds, but "the more you watched Jack Mildren play the more admiration you had for him," said Oklahoma offensive tackle Dean Unruh. "In the wishbone he took just an unbelievable beating. He knew he was going to get hit every play, and he never got hurt, never complained. Just got up and did his job. A great leader. During games you're busy doing your job, and then you go and watch the game film the next day and the first time you see each play you're watching yourself to see what you did good and what you did bad. On the second go-through, you'd watch Mildren pitch the football and watch him get hit by both defensive ends—one from the front side and one from the back side—and just make a perfect pitch out to Pruitt or whomever and off they'd go. Jack would just get up and walk back to the huddle. And you'd just see him making play after play, and slipping tackles. A terrific player to have on your team. A great competitor who did whatever it took to win."

Mildren was a senior, and Crosswhite (6' 2", 203), Pruitt (5' 9", 176), and Wylie (6' 1", 185) were all juniors. Combined, they were the most lethal rushing backfield ever to step on a football field. There was some sense this might be the case before the season started. "We were excited going into that year because of the wishbone Mr. Switzer put in and the results we had the year before," said Leon Crosswhite. "Even though it was new, we knew we were going to be good the next year. The first year that my class showed up down there, the freshman coach and Barry Switzer got us together and said, 'You're the second group of guys we've recruited that is the caliber of team that can vie for a national championship.' The first year was Jack Mildren and that group. Then our group was a really excellent recruiting year and we knew it—we had Greg Pruitt and Joe Wylie, and Dean Unruh and Tom Brahaney and all those linemen who were so good." Wylie and Pruitt were from Texas, but Crosswhite, who broke into the starting lineup in the fifth game of the 1970 season with 109 yards on twenty carries against Colorado, was Sooner born and bred.

Crosswhite was from the little farm town of Hennessey, in the central part of the state. "When Oklahoma had games, my dad used to send my little brother and me out to plow and he'd head for the house to listen to the game on radio," said Crosswhite. "We had one of those modern tractors with an enclosure on it. It had a radio and an air conditioner in it. That tractor made so much danged noise you had to turn the radio up real loud. If the game was exciting, I'd just shut her down and listen. When Joe Don Looney won the '62 game against Syracuse with a long run at the end, I got so keyed up I had to cut the motor and listen. Boy oh boy, was I nervous.

"You get used to working," said Crosswhite. "Sometimes we'd plow both day and night, never stop. You'd plow until you got tired and someone else would take over. But that was nothing compared to pitching hay in the barn when it's a hundred and forty degrees. Whew!

"I had an older brother, Rodney, who was six years older than I was. He played cornerback for OU. That's where I wanted to go also, especially since he went there. I was not recruited real heavily because everyone thought I was too slow. And I remember, one day, right before signings—must have been toward the end of January—Rodney came and got me out of class in high school to see Warren Harper, a coach from OU. On the way to the gymnasium Rodney said, 'Look, you've got one chance to make it. They're going to time you in the sixty-yard dash. You gotta do it.' I ran as hard as I could and happened to run a good time. I have no idea what the time was, but Coach Harper turned to my brother and said, 'We're going to take him.'"

When Pruitt was being recruited out of B.C. Elmore High in Houston, there was no question about his speed. They called him Spotlight "because I was always in it," said Pruitt.

Elmore was a favorite recruiting spot for Oklahoma offensive line coach Bill Michael, and he'd had his eyes on Pruitt from the time the player was a quarterback in the ninth grade. Wendell Mosely, the varsity coach at Elmore, was fond of Michael, who was the first white recruiter to visit the school. As an assistant at Texas Western and then Oklahoma, Michael stopped by Elmore nearly a hundred times over a seven-year period and signed nine players from the school, including Albert Qualls and Lionel Day, starters on the Sooner defense in 1971. But it was Pruitt whom Mosely pointed out one day to Michael, saying, "He'll be a great one." Michael saw what everyone else saw—a 5' 7", 140-pound boy.

"You're going to get hurt playing with all those big guys," Michael joked when introduced to Pruitt.

"They can't get their hands on me," said Pruitt.

Pruitt grew an inch and gained ten pounds, and in the tenth grade started as Elmore's varsity quarterback, where he stayed until the second game of his senior year. "They were all ganging up on him," said Mosely. "I had to find a way to get the ball to him more." Mosely moved another fantastic athlete, Dyaine Frazier (later a high school All-American, and eventually a professional baseball player), to quarterback and put Pruitt out as a split end, where he caught eighty-seven passes and scored twenty-seven touchdowns. Those were eye-popping numbers, and the Universities of Arizona, Colorado, and Houston were all interested in making Pruitt a scholarship player. He pre-enrolled at Houston, while Bill Michael was in Norman doing his damnedest to convince Fairbanks to grab Pruitt. "He's the best-looking thing I've ever seen for running ability," said Michael in enlisting the aid of Switzer to land the prize. "Forget about his size."

It wasn't until a week before the national signing date in May that Oklahoma offered Pruitt a ticket to ride. "Greg Pruitt had so much ability it was scary how good he was," said Fairbanks. "But he weighed about a hundred and fifty pounds and we didn't have any film on him. Once he got to Norman, it was clear he was a rare, rare guy. One of the great natural-reflex athletes I ever coached in my life. If he saw something out of his left eye he'd jump straight sideways to the right. Unbelievable ability to change direction, unbelievable ability to accelerate. Terrific confidence in his ability to do things. And he had the marvelous hands to be either a receiver, a kick returner, or a punt returner."

Wylie was considered the most accomplished of the three juniors. He was a highly prized recruit from Texas who was an All–Big Eight selection as a sophomore when he led the Sooners in scoring with thirteen touchdowns, and averaged 6.2 yards per carry for just under 1,000 yards on the season. He was also the team's punter and primary kickoff return man. "If I get to play," said Wylie in a typically self-effacing manner before the season started, "I hope to improve on my blocking. I'm not a very good blocker. When I block, I sorta halfway miss the guy and he sorta halfway trips. I get some ribbing about that." Wylie's GPA at Oklahoma was a perfect 4.0. Incredibly, with one exception, he'd received an A in every class he'd ever taken at every grade level at every school he'd attended. The exception came in sixth grade, when he received a B in an art class.

"Somehow I wasn't very good in art," said Wylie.

EIGHT

The calm confidence of a Christian with four aces.

—Mark Twain

DOWN IN NORMAN, CHUCK FAIRBANKS, HIS YOUNG staff, and their sublimely gifted Sooners impressed people as a group on the brink of being something special. "You can feel it in Norman," said Dick Wade, a visiting writer from the *Kansas City Star*. "They think this team can win the championship. Fairbanks seems to be more confident, and that's a sign of things to come." The Sooners hadn't proved anything to anyone yet, however. In subsequent years the myth evolved that both teams opened the season staring straight across a void to their eventual meeting on Thanksgiving Day. For certain, the Sooners didn't have that luxury, and it just wasn't the Cornhuskers' style. Any talk of an eventual Thanksgiving Day battle, particularly early-season talk, was preceded by a big "If" followed by "Oklahoma can make it through the early part of its schedule."

Up in Lincoln, Devaney and his players welcomed the season with a relaxed confidence that came with having thirty-eight lettermen return from the 1970 national champions. "Today and yesterday are the happiest days of the summer for me," said senior quarterback Jerry Tagge at the start of summer camp. Tagge spoke for thousands of football players over a hundred years, all of them familiar with the return of camaraderie after a summer apart. "It was so good to see everybody coming back to campus and seeing everyone back together again."

After nine seasons at Nebraska, Devaney's record was 79–18–1, and his overall college record was 114–28–6. His winning percentage of .791 was the best of any major-college coach with more than ten years under his belt, and it was suddenly fashionable to refer to Devaney as the winningest coach in the game and then act astonished that he'd won more than Parseghian, McKay, Bryant, Hayes, Royal, and everyone else.

Devaney wore the beginning of his tenth season at Nebraska like a favorite old sweater. "I think we'll have a great attitude this year," Devaney said, looking over the team as it gathered for press photos. "Already some of our players have started to make some tough sacrifices. [Split end] Woody Cox got a haircut so short I didn't recognize him. And [center] Doug Dumler trimmed his mustache. I'd say the squad is starting to get really serious."

On the field, photographers popped off shots of the giant (6' 6", 250) senior defensive tackle Larry Jacobson as he snarled and dived on fake fumbles while wearing the black-rimmed eyeglasses he wore when he wasn't playing football. The photos were straight out of *Attack of the Killer Nerds*, and made it impossible to believe that by season's end Jacobson would win the Outland Trophy as the nation's outstanding lineman. "I wore contacts for a while," said Jacobson, "but then I got knocked out in a game and I got one lost up in my eye. I thought I lost it until two or three days later when my eye started hurting, and the lens had gotten knocked way in the hell up there and they were those hard contacts back then. And I got it out and said, 'Screw this.' I could see who had the ball just fine without my glasses. I just couldn't see the sidelines. I could see fifteen feet or so and that's all I needed to see to be a lineman. When I won the Outland Trophy, I'd never even heard of it. I had to get [defensive coordinator] Monte Kiffin to spell it for me."

Devaney could afford to joke because he knew his players had a workmanlike attitude about football, and that they adored him. He'd been at Nebraska long enough that some of the players on the squad remembered him from their early boyhood years, and were grateful that it was Devaney who created the impression that Nebraska was more than some wild frontier outpost.

Mike Beran, a backup offensive lineman on the 1971 team and a starter the following year, recalled the first time he ever met Devaney. "I'm originally from a town called Ord," said Beran. "It's right out in the center of the state, about fifty miles north of Grand Island. There are about 2,500 people in Ord, so it's not real big. When I was a sophomore in high school I was in Lincoln watching the state basketball tournament. I was just walking down the street with some friends and we passed Coach Devaney. He said 'Hi,' to us all and, well, he was a godlike figure in Nebraska. The impression that he left on me by taking the time to say hello to three or four high school kids was really something.

"I remember when Coach Devaney was first hired," said Beran. "People were down, and there were a lot of expectations when Coach Devaney first came along. He was the talk of the town—talk of the state, actually. When Coach Devaney came to Nebraska the whole state caught the football fever. Basically, he put the state on the map. I can still remember going to the Washington, D.C., area in 1963 to see some of my cousins back there, and they seriously still thought that we fought the Indians and still rode around in covered wagons. That was the East Coast's view of Nebraska. But after Coach Devaney came and the football team succeeded everyone knew about Nebraska. I just wanted to be a part of that."

Senior running back Jeff Kinney grew up in McCook, a town of about 8,000 people out toward the southwest corner of Nebraska, where it forms a right angle with Kansas and Colorado. "Coach Devaney really had a great way of relating to young men," said Kinney. "He knew the right words to say at the right time. Coach Osborne recruited me, and he was a straight shooter. He told you the truth, and sometimes you didn't like it, but he always told you the truth. I was impressed with his serious approach and had just about made up my mind to go to Nebraska."

Vince Gibson, the gregarious coach of Kansas State, wasn't

about to let Kinney go to Lincoln without a fight. "My mom liked the Kansas State approach," said Kinney. "They really put on the dog. My folks were taken out to dinner several times and I must honestly say I really thought seriously of going to Manhattan [Kansas]." Someone was always knocking on the Kinney family's front door in McCook. Coaches from Texas, Tennessee, and UCLA stopped by, among others. In the end, the deciding factor for Kinney was Devaney. "I liked Coach Devaney and had been to a few games in Lincoln. Those Nebraska fans are the greatest." When Devaney arrived in McCook for Kinney to sign his national letter of intent "it was like entertaining the president of the United States," Kinney said. "I think most Nebraskans would feel the same way.

"There was a lot of expectations placed upon us at the start of 1971," said Kinney. "To be honest, one of the things that made us unique was that it seemed like every week we didn't really care who we played. We looked forward to the opportunity to go out and demonstrate the kind of football team that we were. In the time and place where I grew up, the head coach was someone you revered and respected. We always sought Coach Devaney's approval, and the best way to get that was to play hard."

"We had total confidence going into 1971," said Bill Kosch, who was a senior safety on the team, "but not arrogance. Our team was not arrogant, not ever. There weren't guys shooting their mouths off, talking about what we were going to do three games ahead. We were guardedly cautious. We saw teams get beat, knew upsets happened, and knew it could happen to us, so we were determined not to let it happen. We were very businesslike and well conditioned, and prepared extremely hard for each game. I think our edge was in mental preparation. There were never any surprises."

The team voted for seniors Jerry Tagge and Jim Anderson, the old friends from Green Bay, as their captains. "Jerry and I went to the same high school," said Anderson years later, "and we were fairly successful in both football and, actually, more successful in basketball a little more than football. I played point guard, and he played forward. Jerry was a great basketball player, a great shooter. And I just played defense. I'm a year older than Jerry, but we finished up at Nebraska in the same year because I redshirted one year and he didn't.

"We had a pretty motivated group in 1971," said Anderson, who started more games in his career at Nebraska than anyone else on the team. In 1969 and '70, Anderson had played 802 minutes of football for the Huskers. "My leadership style was pretty low-key. Basically a leadership by example kind of thing. I didn't do a lot of talking to get people pumped up, or to have them do this or that. Our team was pretty keyed in on everybody doing their own job."

"It makes me the most grateful person in the world to realize these guys think enough of you to vote you their captain," said Tagge, who at the time was the holder of nine school records in total offense, and poised to become the first Nebraska quarterback ever to throw for more than 3,000 yards in his career.

The official stand by Devaney before the first game was that seniors Tagge and Van Brownson would alternate at quarterback, and it was no joke when Devaney said the Huskers could win with either man at the wheel. Brownson started three games in the national championship season of 1970, and completed 49 of 75 passes and rang up 6 touchdowns. But in spring practice, Brownson separated his shoulder. Even though Brownson was healthy for the '71 season, the offense clearly belonged to Tagge as long as he performed well enough to suit Devaney. If neither Tagge nor Brownson could get the job done, said Devaney, he'd go with sophomore Dave Humm, who had shattered every freshman record in the Husker book.

The fever was spreading.

A sculptor in Maywood, Illinois, created a clay bust of Bob Devaney, complete with baseball-style cap tilted far back on the forehead in the style of the coach. The likeness was eerie, and Richard Shonka, the sculptor, appealed to Nebraska followers for funds so that the next step could be taken to "reproduce [the work] into the imperishable medium of granite and presented in its fullness to Bob Devaney or the University of Nebraska for permanent installation in a proper setting."

Devaney wrote back to Shonka, "You obviously put a lot of work into this, and you certainly do a fine job."

As the start of classes approached there were 140 intramural football teams that students could play on at Lincoln. At Natelsons Department Store, any $30 charge was good for a free "We're No. 1 Nebraska" stadium cushion. A total of $200 in a savings account at Nebraska Savings was worth a two-inch-thick "Go Big Red" stadium cushion (red and white, of course) *and* an all-weather "Go Big Red" poncho. The same amount in an account at First National Bank of Omaha netted a folding stadium seat with a back (but no "Go Big Red") *or* a cozy red stadium blanket complete with "Go Big Red" in white letters. To sweeten the pot, depositors at First National were registered to win a trip for two to Nebraska's final regular-season game against the University of Hawaii. T-shirts with a 1 in the center and the word NEBRASKA cutting across the numeral were available in gray, red, or white for $3. Children's sizes were $2.50; a sweatshirt was $4.50. For $7 a Husker fan could purchase 200 "Go Big Red" and "Nebraska #1" self-stick paper badges, red on white. Stores set aside entire departments for Big Red merchandise. Goodrich Dairy in Omaha marketed "Go Big Red" milk with the slogan, "Now here's a great new way to support Big Red." McKee Farms, in Clay Center, Kansas, sent "Go Big Red" eggs to market. Brandeis Department Store offered a handmade Swiss music box that played the school song, "No Place Like Nebraska." When the order for 1,000 boxes was placed with the Swiss firm, the store sent along the sheet music because the music box maker had never heard of the song and couldn't find the music to it.

Expatriate Nebraskans could get coverage of every Husker

game in the mail via the *Omaha World-Herald* for $4.75 in Iowa or anywhere within 300 miles of Omaha. At 600 miles from Omaha the price was $5.40, and in the rest of the U.S. it was $6.05. Servicemen and women on active duty anywhere in the world could receive the newspaper's Big Red Care Package. A mail-order display ad for Magee's, in Lincoln, trumpeted the Big Red Stomper stadium boot, made from Go-Big-Red suede with white rope lacing, white crepe soles, and white stitching. At the bottom of the ad was a reminder: "Don't Miss Part I of 'The Devaney Years' on Wednesday, September 1, 7:30 on KETV–Channel 7 and KHOL-TV, Channel 13."

The classified ads in the Sunday newspaper carried an entry for a "1970 four-door sedan, custom model, power steering, power brakes and air conditioning." The asking price was $3,200 and included two season tickets to Nebraska home games. The man's phone rang off the hook, with most people interested solely in the tickets, not the car. Another ad offered a straight-up swap: two season tickets to the Kansas City Chiefs for two Nebraska season tickets.

Nebraska's ticket manager, Jim Pittenger, was having some long days. There were 62,800 seats available in Memorial Stadium. There were 31,000 season-ticket holders and the students accounted for another 20,000 tickets. Faculty and employees gobbled up 7,800 tickets per game, and visiting teams were granted a maximum allotment of 3,000 tickets. That left only 1,000 available tickets for each home game. Pittenger spent so much office time on the phone with people angling for tickets that he ended up doing all of his work at home at night. There were two solutions to the ticket squeeze as Pittenger saw it: a losing season, or a bigger stadium.

For all those fans who couldn't get inside Memorial Stadium for home games there were only two televised games on the schedule: Colorado on October 30, and Oklahoma on November 25, Thanksgiving Day. Both were the national game of the week on the ABC network. For the other games, ticketless fans would tune in to KFAB on their radios and listen to the rapid-fire call of the "voice of the Cornhuskers," Lyell Bremser, who was in his thirty-third season behind the microphone. Nebraska fans would know a play was going their way when they heard Bremser holler either of his trademark phrases, "Holy Toledo!" or "Man, Woman, and Child!"

"Coach Devaney was kind of easy on us during training camp," recalled Jeff Kinney. "I remember saying to him, 'Coach, I need to have some contact. I need to get hit a few times here.' He was more concerned about us getting hurt than he was about doing any specific drills. During the season, we never had any contact at all. I was the kind of running back that just felt like the more licks I got the stronger I got. I needed to feel like I was getting hit to get into game-playing shape."

With the season drawing near, Devaney let his assistants handle the nitty-gritty of contact drills. During the halfway break in each practice the team drank a saltwater solution mixed with ice and ate wedges of oranges. Sharp-eyed trainers across the country had noticed a few years earlier that Astroturf and other synthetic surfaces heated up like a skillet in the hot August sun, often registering on-field temperatures twenty degrees higher than the air temperature. To combat the intensified heat, Devaney ordered the field hosed down.

"I think that a lot of [Coach Devaney's] success can be attributed to the type of assistants he had," said Mike Beran. "He was a good organizer. He would walk around and go from station to station—that's what we called them. Say the defense was working at one station on a particular play or a particular defense they were going to run. At another station the offense would work on plays we were going to run. Coach Devaney would walk between those stations and offer advice and tell the players a few things, tell the coaches what he wanted. He might yell occasionally, but mainly he left the criticism and a lot of the praise to his assistant coaches.

"Our offensive line coaches were Carl Selmer and Cletus Fischer," said Beran. "Carl Selmer was more like Tom Osborne. He had kind of a quiet demeanor—very scholarly type of individual. Coach Fischer was the one who did more vocalization. He had this saying, 'You've got to get in there and root-hog!' In other words, get your nose down, keep your head low. Don't come off the ball high, stay down, you can do better. Every time a play would start during scrimmage, Coach Fischer would say, 'Get up the field! Get up the field!' He was yelling at the running back to get down the field with the ball and the linemen to be there with him to make another block. I can still hear him saying, 'You've got to root-hog!'"

Mike Corgan, a hard-nosed merchant marine during World War II, coached the offensive backs. Corgan had been on Devaney's staff at Wyoming and followed his boss to Nebraska. If Devaney was cautious about getting his key players banged up in practice, Corgan had no such reservations. "He is one of the toughest men on earth," said Kinney at the time. "He has no respect for second-raters. He taught me how to block and turn the corner. The one thing he demanded was that even though we were carrying the ball we should deliver the blow."

On the defensive side of the ball, defensive coordinator and former Husker player Monte Kiffin was a player favorite. In later years, Kiffin became a revered defensive coordinator in the National Football League, coaching the attack of the 2003 Super Bowl champion Tampa Bay Buccaneers, among others. "We had an excellent coaching staff," said Bill Kosch. "I think the key to that was the variety of personalities. Monte Kiffin lived football. He lived, breathed, and ate football. You'd see him walking around on campus after practice, and all of a sudden he'd stop in his tracks, and his eyes would roll up in his head and then he'd take off walking again. He must have been solving some sort of defensive scheme or breaking down an offense. Just constantly thinking about or talking about football.

"I remember a scrimmage one time," said Kosch, "and the fourth string—we called them the greenshirts—and they were out there having a scrimmage. Kiffin would coach them just as hard as the varsity. Somebody fumbled and the ball was rolling toward the sidelines, and Monte Kiffin recovered it. He beat some offensive guy to the ball. He was totally into it. Our defensive-back coach Warren Powers had professional experience [six years with the Oakland Raiders] and had played for the Cornhuskers. He taught us a lot of good techniques. John Melton, the linebacker coach, always had a cigar in his mouth. You'd get in a film session with him and you'd watch, say, Jerry Murtaugh make a perfect hit, just clean somebody's clock. And John would get mesmerized and just keep going back and forth. You'd have to shake him and say, 'Show the rest of the game!' It was a good cross-section of brains, enthusiasm, and personalities."

Jacobson was particularly fond of Kiffin, who had recruited him out of O'Gorman Catholic in Sioux Falls, South Dakota. "We were 0–7–1 when I was a junior and 8–1 my senior year," said Jacobson. "The coaches from Nebraska were recruiting a kid from a Sioux City school that we played up in Sioux Falls, and it was one of the best games I ever played. And they stopped recruiting him and started recruiting me. I got recruited by Monte Kiffin and Bob Devaney. Back then they had conference letters of intent and two national letters of intent, one for the guys who were just football players, and one for the guys who played two sports. I played basketball in high school, also, and got recruited by some smaller schools for basketball.

"I went down to Nebraska for some visits after all the basketball tournaments finished," said Jacobson. "I knew some kids from my school who'd gone down there. They didn't play football or anything, but when I went down on recruiting trips I'd always kind of ditch the players they had sit with us, and I'd just go out with my friends. The last two times I was down there, Devaney gave me his wife's car to drive around while I was there. I was a little kid coming from a small school and here they gave me a red Bonneville convertible to drive around in, which I thought was kinda cool.

"I signed a letter of intent with Iowa to play in the Big Ten," said

Jacobson, "and then I signed one with Nebraska. When I called the coach at Iowa to tell him I thought I was going to Nebraska, he wouldn't accept that I wasn't going to Iowa, so he sent one of his coaches up to my high school for the national letter of intent day to try to get me. I was with Monte Kiffin when the guy from Iowa got there, so Monte and I just drove away out the back parking lot of the school. The other coach started following us. So then Kiffin just lost him in traffic—just ditched him—and this guy ended up at my parents' house sitting there for about an hour.

"Well, the guy from Iowa left my parents' house but said he'd come back that night," said Jacobson. "So while I was talking to him, Monte Kiffin was talking to my mom and dad. And the guy from Iowa was kind of shaking my conviction to go to Nebraska. My head was spinning. You have to remember I was just eighteen. Finally Monte said, 'You're still signing the letter aren't you? Because Devaney told me if I don't sign you I can't come back.'

"In the end," said Jacobson, "I wanted to go to a big enough school where I could play major college, but not so far away that my parents couldn't come down to the games. And that's only about 220 miles or so from Sioux Falls to Lincoln.

"Kiffin was crazy. Absolutely nuts. We used to do grass drills, where we'd run in place and hit the ground and bounce back up, and all camp we'd try to do more than we did the year before. And the last day in camp, we'd try to set the record for the next year and Monte would get out in front and do them with us. One of the other defensive coaches was Thunder Thornton, and the last time we got out there to do the grass drills, Monte did them all but Thunder laid on the ground for the last ten, he couldn't get back up. We heard stories about him from when he was a player and he was a little crazy. He was from Lexington, Nebraska, and lived and died the game. He's the one who taught me to be persistent and never give up."

The defensive unit Kiffin coached was known as the Blackshirts, a nickname it picked up from the color of the jerseys worn by its starting eleven during practice. The tradition began early in the Devaney years when the coach sent two assistants to a sporting goods store to buy some practice jerseys. The black ones were the cheapest. The shirts quickly took on a strong symbolic meaning. Defensive teams at other schools even copied the trend, but there was and always would be one group of Blackshirts.

"At Nebraska that [black shirt] is the biggest thing you can get as far as a team or a group of guys," said Jacobson. " We all kind of hung together and it was really nice. Nowadays they make a big deal about it, but back then when you made the first team they just gave you a black shirt."

"It evolved into a thing of pretty intense pride over the years to be on that Blackshirt defense," said Jim Anderson. "We enhanced the mystique and put it on the map with our defenses in 1970 and '71."

As the drilling continued leading up to September 11 and the opening game against Oregon, Kiffin said "our pass rush could be the best we've ever had here." Offensive lines that the Huskers would meet in the coming weeks would find it hard to argue.

"I think there is a certain amount of pressure on the squad after winning the Big Eight, the Orange Bowl, and the national championship last season," said Devaney on the last day of August. "Everybody is a little more tense and anxious. As coaches, we're more critical than in the past when we judge performances in scrimmages—more critical than we have a right to be. Any problems we're having certainly aren't due to fatheadedness on the part of the players. I have no argument whatsoever with the effort or enthusiasm."

On September 4, one week prior to Nebraska's opener, the Associated Press preseason poll was released. A first-place vote was worth twenty points, a second-place vote eighteen. In descending order from third place on down, votes had point values of sixteen, fourteen, twelve, ten, nine, eight, etc. A panel of fifty writers and broadcasters across the country voted, and twenty-six picked

Nebraska as number one. Fifteen picked Notre Dame as number one, and another twenty-five picked the Irish as number two. Of the twenty-four voters who didn't pick Nebraska number one, only ten selected them as the number two team. The result was that Notre Dame was the AP pick for number one, with 885 votes. Nebraska was second, with 870 votes.

Not a down had been played, of course, and Bob Devaney knew it. "It's nice to be picked up there high," said Devaney, "and it's better to have people thinking well of you than badly, but the ones [polls] at the end of the season are the ones that count. I'm certain our players would like to be number one, but I don't think at this stage it has any great psychological effect."

The remainder of the AP preseason top ten was rounded out by (in order) Texas, Michigan, Southern Cal, Auburn, Arkansas, Tennessee, LSU, and Oklahoma.

When the thirty-five members of the UPI coaches' poll released their preseason votes, Nebraska received twenty-five first-place nods and the number one ranking well ahead of Notre Dame. UPI picked Oklahoma as the ninth-best team. The same week *Sports Illustrated*'s annual college preview hit newsstands with Notre Dame as its choice for the best college team in the country. The sports weekly picked Nebraska as its number two squad, and Oklahoma the seventeenth best without even mentioning the name of Greg Pruitt.

When the Highland Country Club held a coaches' stag outing for Devaney and his staff, host pro Jerry Dugan and his pro shop assistants greeted the Nebraska coaches wearing Notre Dame jerseys with the number 1 on them. Devaney played along with the gag and posed for pictures with the kids. It didn't put him off his game at all. Devaney shot an 85, beating defensive back coach Warren Powers by two strokes and Tom Osborne by three.

NINE

The heights by great men reached and kept
Were not attained by sudden flight,
But they, while their companions slept
Were toiling upward in the night.

—Henry Wadsworth Longfellow,
"The Ladder of St. Augustine"

1971 Schedules

	NEBRASKA	OKLAHOMA
Sept. 11	Oregon (H)	No game
Sept. 18	Minnesota (H)	Southern Methodist (H)
Sept. 25	Texas A&M (H)	Pittsburgh
Oct. 2	Utah State (H)	Southern California (H)
Oct. 9	Missouri	Texas (in Dallas)
Oct. 16	Kansas (H)	Colorado (H)
Oct. 23	Oklahoma State	Kansas State
Oct. 30	Colorado (H)	Iowa State (H)
Nov. 6	Iowa State (H)	Missouri
Nov. 13	Kansas State	Kansas (H)
Nov. 25	Oklahoma	Nebraska (H)
Dec. 4	Hawaii	Oklahoma State

Nebraska opened defense of its national title against the Oregon Ducks, who were quarterbacked by future National Football League hall of famer Dan Fouts. Out on the West Coast, in the

113

Pacific Eight Conference, Fouts was correctly viewed (as history later showed) as a player with all the tools to make it in the pro ranks. Furthermore, Fouts could place the ball in the hands of Bobby Moore, a devastating runner and receiver who would later have an all-pro career for the Minnesota Vikings.

Nebraska's defense was too mighty for the two offensive dynamos from the coast, however, and the Cornhuskers methodically rolled to a 34–7 win. It was the twentieth consecutive game without a loss for Nebraska. The Cornhusker defense completely throttled the potent Duck offense, and Nebraska's first three scores came after sustained marches of 67, 47, and 99 yards. The Husker defense shut out the Ducks until a fumbled punt deep in Nebraska territory set up a 7-yard scoring run by Moore. Fouts was harassed all day by the defense and was off-target with many of his throws.

Jerry Tagge, the more accomplished but less renowned of the two quarterbacks in the game, executed the option perfectly time and time again, and hit on eight of ten passes for 98 yards to set the school's career passing-yardage mark with a total of 2,989 yards.

Jeff Kinney had 124 yards on twenty-two carries, while the Blackshirts held Moore to 53 yards in fifteen tries. Fouts was intercepted three times, generally found his receivers well-covered, and was forced on several occasions to dump the ball off to secondary receivers for short gains.

"The Nebraska defense is dynamite," said Moore after the game. "They are all real quick and they don't make mistakes."

"That's as good of a defense as I've ever seen," said Fouts. "Their safeties played tighter than I expected. It looked like our receivers had trouble getting open."

With the win over Oregon, Nebraska was immediately elevated to the number one spot in the Associated Press weekly poll released the following Monday. Notre Dame's preseason reign hadn't even lasted until their first game.

One week later, the Cornhuskers hosted the Minnesota Golden

Gophers. Nebraska totaled 421 yards in total offense on the day, and won handily, 35–7. Jeff Kinney scored two touchdowns on the ground. For a brief moment before the half, with the score 14–7, it seemed as if Minnesota might tie the game. They had the ball on the Husker ten-yard line, but failed to capitalize. When asked after the game if that was the turning point in the game, Minnesota head coach Murray Warmath laughed and said, "The turning point was when the referee blew the whistle for the opening kickoff."

Dick Tannahill, who was at the game scouting the Huskers for Utah State, said, "I'm glad I don't have to come up with all the answers. All I have to do is come up with the problems."

Jim Keller, a Texas A&M freshman coach who was scouting Nebraska for the second week in a row, said, "A week ago I charted one of the top ground-gaining teams. Now today they used the pass. I knew they could use it anytime they wanted to. Johnny Rodgers is a real game-breaker. I'd say he's as exciting a football player as there is in the country. But he's not the whole offense. Jerry Tagge is very calm and throws well. And there's another thing. Tagge had time to throw. Those blockers aren't just good for the ground game, they protect their passer well."

George Nash, a Minnesota assistant who scouted the Huskers a week earlier against Oregon, left the press box shaking his head and saying, "They did it again." After stopping Minnesota when the Gophers could have tied the score, Tagge led the Huskers 80 yards in seven plays for a touchdown and 21–7 halftime lead. On the drive, Tagge passed to Jerry List for 22 yards, hit Jeff Kinney for another 15, and split end Woody Cox for 17 more. Kinney started the drive with a 3-yard run, and ended it by covering the final 10 yards in two of his trademark lumberjack carries. "When we didn't score and they turned around and drove it the length of the field on us, that was the backbreaker," said Nash. "But then again, that's the sign of a great team."

It was a sign, as well, that Nebraska could move the ball at will, and shut down opposing offenses when they threatened to score. It was a distinct pattern. Nebraska was so much better than they had been the previous season, they would not be fully tested until they met Oklahoma.

On September 18, the Sooners opened at home in the rain for the first time since 1936. Their opponent was Southern Methodist University. With all the talk about the Sooner offense, it was the Oklahoma defense that ruled the day in a 30–0 shutout. Southern Methodist only managed to move the ball across the fifty-yard line twice in the entire game, and when they did, they never got closer to the Sooner goal line than twenty-nine yards. John Carroll, a rookie kicker, booted field goals of 33, 25, and 43 yards. Greg Pruitt, Jack Mildren, and Leon Crosswhite added the touchdowns. On one particularly stellar defensive series, Raymond "Sugar Bear" Hamilton, the quick-footed end, threw SMU quarterback Gary Hammond for consecutive losses of 3 and 9 yards, and then tackled him for no gain.

The Sooner offense displayed its quick-strike ability the following weekend against the University of Pittsburgh. The first time a Sooner touched the ball, it was Joe Wylie on a kick return. The next time a Sooner touched the ball, it was to snap the ball for the extra point, because Wylie sped 85 yards for a touchdown with that kickoff. The Sooners ran off thirty-two plays on their next six possessions and rushed for 379 yards. That was an average of 11.8 yards per carry.

Pitt's game plan was to control the ball and pound the middle of the Sooner defense while mixing in some short passes. The Panther attack was successful, but the twenty-nine points it produced were not even in the neighborhood of what they needed. Oklahoma was simply unstoppable, eventually racking up 567 total yards, with 418 of them coming on fifty rushing attempts. Mildren completed six of nine attempts throwing for 149 yards. Mildren and Wylie each scored three touchdowns, Pruitt scored once, and so did Tim Welch, the backup fullback. The final score was 55–29 in favor of Oklahoma.

"We might have watched the number one team in the country today," said one writer in attendance. "Boy, what a game that'll be when Oklahoma plays Texas." Pitt Coach Carl DePasqua said after the game, "Oklahoma is the most explosive, and has the best offensive machine, I've ever seen. As far as I'm concerned, with the system they have, Jack Mildren is the finest quarterback I've ever seen. His pitches are just fantastic. They are done with timing and precision, and are done based on how he reads the defense."

Fairbanks wasn't happy with his defense. "We did not play defense well today," said the coach. "To have the season we want to have, we must have good play in all phases."

When one writer asked Fairbanks if he felt it was possible for his team to contend for the number one spot in the national polls, Fairbanks didn't hesitate and was unusually forthright, at least in terms of talking to the press. "Yes," said Fairbanks. "It's possible for us to be number one."

Oklahoma had won the first two of its four critical opening games. The next week they welcomed the University of Southern California to Norman. The USC team was loaded to the gills with first-line players such as running back Sam "Bam" Cunningham and wide receiver Lynn Swann.

The game proved to be a most frustrating one for the Trojans' legendary coach, John McKay. "Our defensive players weren't where I wanted them," said McKay. "When I got them where I wanted them they got blocked. When they weren't getting blocked, they missed the tackles. Oklahoma was superior, we were inferior."

Up on the scoreboard the source of all McKay's misery was in full view. His team had managed just 20 points to Oklahoma's 33. "I think Oklahoma has a fine team," said McKay. "But when a guy runs downfield and eight guys miss him on a tackle like happened with Pruitt, that's our fault."

Other defenders would soon discover that Pruitt was a tough customer to get a handle on. "I kidded Wylie and Pruitt all week," said Barry Switzer after the game, "by telling them they could have new jerseys for today's game. They were going to say 'Hello' on the front, and 'Goodbye' on the back."

And so was born the T-shirt that Greg Pruitt wore in so many photos in so many newspapers.

Fairbanks's team had opened with three straight knockouts. The Sooners rushed for nearly 516 yards against USC, and didn't gain a single yard through the air. The Sooners led at halftime 19–14, but Pruitt broke the game open with a 75-yard scoring run with five minutes left in the third quarter. "Our offensive line just blocked super," said Jack Mildren. "When we get outside it's all over."

Switzer was surprised that Pruitt and Wylie could get wide with such ease. "I didn't think we'd be able to run the corners like we did," said Switzer. "But it's nothing for backs to run up into the holes our offensive line was making."

"It was a great day for all of us," said Fairbanks. "Now we've got to start getting ready for those 'Horns tomorrow. And that's not going to be an easy job."

The game that vaulted the 1971 Oklahoma Sooners from possibly great to unquestionably so was played against the third-ranked Texas Longhorns at the Texas State Fairgrounds in Dallas, on October 9, in front of 73,580 people.

"In the '71 game against Texas, we were the dominant team," said Jack Mildren of the 48–27 Oklahoma victory. "It was obvious that we were so much faster and quicker than they were. That game was a defining moment for us. Without a doubt it signaled a return of the Sooners to the national spotlight."

Darrell Royal described Oklahoma's defense as "quick and aggressive" and the team overall as "strong": "They've got talent, they are confident. They have it all going for them right now, like high water over level ground. Or maybe it's downhill ground."

It was the end of a five-year winless streak against Texas, and it was the first time a Chuck Fairbanks–led Sooner team had beaten Darrell Royal's boys.

As the clock expired, with the eighth-ranked Sooners assured a win, the packed Cotton Bowl echoed with the unrestrained glee of "We're number one!" and "It's on to the Orange Bowl for us!"

The public address announcer urged the ecstatic fans to keep clear of the playing field, but when the gun sounded the throng surged onto the battleground, and a delirious mob of Oklahomans engaged in the time-honored tradition of attempting to rip down the goalposts. A Dallas policeman watching the scene shook his head and said, "I don't want to try to stop them. A miracle has happened here today. And who can try to prevent the aftermath of a miracle."

A taxicab driver stopping near the stadium said, "If there are any Oklahomans here, I'll take them for free. I don't think I could afford to charge them after what has happened in the Cotton Bowl. It may take a long time for this to really sink in, but you folks from across the Red River have really got something, and we've got to bow down to you neighbors."

Jim Blue, a public relations man for the University of Oklahoma, paced like an expectant father up and down the sidelines and said, "Is this really true? Have we *really* beaten Texas?"

Outside the stadium, another police officer predicted a wild time in the old town of Dallas that night. "They said the Longhorns couldn't be beaten," said the lawman, "but it looks like it has happened now. I hate to think what tonight will bring. I reckon we'll brace ourselves for a real crazy time."

When the game ended, the Sooners' mascot, Little Red, did a war dance at one end of the green Astroturf. He pulled out his tomahawk and let out a gigantic war cry. "We really clamped a teepee over these Texans!"

"I knew it was going to happen," said an Episcopal priest from Norman, who had arrived in that town just two years earlier after fifteen years as a Texas fan. This season, when he flew into Dallas, he wore a red shirt beneath his clerical collar. He also wore red socks. "I've been converted," the minister said.

When the Sooners arrived at the Will Rogers World Airport back in Oklahoma, the noise of the plane was just a background hum to the louder thunder of adoring fans waiting to greet the conquering heroes after the sweetest victory in five years and maybe longer. The fans stormed the airport and filled up every available parking space, and clogged traffic. The crowd, estimated by police to be 5,000 strong, began piling into the airport at 6:00 P.M., not even an hour after the game's final gun. Airport officials set up a speaker stand, and one fan, who said he worked in an electrical shop, had a speaker mounted on the roof of his car. When the big plane landed, the chaos was too much for both the police and airport security. The noisy mob stormed the speaker stand and surrounded the plane, cheering wildly. Police escorted a smiling Fairbanks and his squad to waiting buses, amid cheers of "We're number one!" and "We want Chuck!"

Everywhere people carried signs that read, "We Beat Texas!" and "GO OU!" and "Beat Colorado!"

Colorado was the next opponent for the Sooners, and a severe test at that. But the win over Texas had dramatically shaken up the landscape of the college game.

When the Associated Press poll came out the following Monday, the Sooners' decisive 48–27 trouncing of Texas vaulted Oklahoma into second place behind Nebraska. The new poll set up the possible Thanksgiving Day showdown everyone had been anticipating.

Both teams rolled through the rest of their schedules, destined for their appointment on Thanksgiving Day.

TEN

For now sits Expectation in the air.

—*Henry V*, by William Shakespeare

FOR PLAYERS FROM BOTH NEBRASKA AND OKLAHOMA, the spectacle of the game they were scheduled to play on Thanksgiving Day was something they had never experienced before. The game was to be televised nationally on ABC on a national holiday at a time of year when most people stayed indoors. There was no cable television, satellite television, or dedicated twenty-four-hour sports programming to compete with the telecast. In fact, television was still enough of a novelty that stores who sold the appliances ran huge advertisements in newspapers that appealed to the possibility of buying a new set so the game could be viewed in *color*, and noted that the big game would be "televised in color on Thanksgiving Day."

"The other two networks [NBC and CBS] did the pro games," said Neil Amdur, who covered the game for the *New York Times*. "ABC had the colleges and made a big fuss over that and they really beat the publicity drum. That was a time period where there was a lot of big college games that took on real meaning, in part because the public was geared more toward one national game than toward fractional regional games. There was a terrific amount of public relations put out by ABC at the time that affected the way college football was looked at, so there was a lot of excitement that way.

"Also," said Amdur, "the pro game is bigger today then it was in the sixties and early seventies, and the college game was much closer to the pro game in terms of popularity. The Super Bowl was still a very new thing, and I think the colleges in that sense probably had much bigger followings than pro teams. And the college coaches at the time were very large figures in the national sporting landscape. Guys like Woody Hayes, Darrell Royal, Bear Bryant, John McKay, and Ara Parseghian were really very high-profile people in sports. *Sports Illustrated* and national publications were not as under the influence of the professional leagues and newspapers tended to give more benefit to college sports than they do now. College sports still had that old-boy-network feel that continued to exist before the pros started going into a lot of new markets."

Amdur was part of the media invasion that descended upon Norman the week of the game. "[Oklahoma sports information director] Johnny Keith arranged for me to meet Jack Mildren at a campus hangout called the Crossroads restaurant, and Jack had his fiancée with him. So here I had an opportunity to do a one-on-one for a Thursday game on a Monday or Tuesday night. That is almost unheard of today in a lot of these games where the players are off-limits except for mass interviews."

The story that Amdur filed for the *Times* was headlined: MILDREN PREDICTS VICTORY: QUARTERBACK CONFIDENT ON EVE OF BIG EIGHT SHOWDOWN WITH NO. 1 NEBRASKA. "I really think we're going to win," Mildren told Amdur and every reader of the *New York Times* sports section. "Our coaches and fans are tighter than the players."

"We understood the stakes," said Mildren years later, "and we liked the attention. We got along with the press, probably said some things that we shouldn't have. As a general rule, we were not a shy group. We didn't think we were tolerating the press; we enjoyed the back and forth. There were five or so beat writers from the local papers, but when it came time for Nebraska it went from five to twenty-five or fifty, so the scrutiny was turned up. In my little world things were the same. I still lived in Washington House [one of the athletic dormitories on campus], same room, same roommate, same girlfriend. Still went to class. My little world of dorm to class to football stadium for practice really didn't change much. Things still moved at our pace, if you will."

Amdur had company in town: There would be ninety-seven writers covering the game, representing sixty-five newspapers, *Sports Illustrated* and *Newsweek*, and the two big wire services, United Press International and the Associated Press. "We had to start turning down newspaper requests last week," said John Keith. "Twenty-some-odd papers have been denied requests because we just don't have the room." The Oklahoma football network was preparing to feed fifty-five radio stations, including outlets in St. Louis, Houston, Honolulu, and Fairbanks, Alaska. The Nebraska football network would carry the game on another fifty radio stations.

ABC was predicting 80 million television viewers in the U.S. "We'll eat the pros alive," said ABC publicist Beano Cook. "This will be one of the most-watched games of all time." In addition, Western Union would beam the game live and in color via satellite to four feed lines in the Pacific that would serve Alaska, Hawaii, Korea, and the Philippines; in the Atlantic, three feed lines would serve Germany, Panama, and Puerto Rico. In Mexico City, Sooner fans would rally at the Ritz Hotel, one of the few hotels in all of Mexico with in-room televisions. True Sooner fans living in Mexico knew that a station in the city carried all ABC games of the week.

As the game drew near, even geeks turned into prognosticators. At Union Pacific in Omaha, an IBM 360 Model 50 predicted a six-point victory for Nebraska. Another computer in North Platte predicted a 31–21 Cornhusker win. Curiously, a computer in Tulsa figured Oklahoma to win, 39–33. In Vegas, Jimmy "The Greek" Snyder gave a slight edge to Nebraska and said, "The secret to Nebraska's winning this football game is to keep Greg Pruitt from going outside." It seemed *everyone* was compelled to weigh in.

In both states, governors and senators declared "Beat The

Other Team" days. The weeks previous to the game were marked by pep rallies, bands, signs, and raised mannequins of players. After waffling on the subject, President Nixon sent word that he was officially unable to make it to Norman for the big game. The nervous state of the general public was summed up beautifully in a cartoon in the *Omaha World-Herald*. A football marked "Go Big Red" sat on top of the television. Uniformed players were on the screen, and a husband clutching a "Nebraska #1" pennant sat with his face buried in his free hand. "What do you mean, you can't look?" said his wife. "That was just the coin toss."

The looming game held the potential to be the greatest ever for several reasons, not least of which was the legacy of Oklahoma's team and its significance to its state contrasted with the emerging excellence of Nebraska's program and *its* significance to *its* state. The pride in Nebraska was something that lived deep within the players. When some of the members of the '71 varsity squad were freshmen, they fell behind in a game to Missouri while Devaney was in the stands watching, waiting for the game to end so the varsity could practice. After opening an 18–0 lead, the freshmen fell behind 23–18. Devaney quietly fumed in the bleachers until he could stand it no more. He stomped down to the sidelines. "What the hell is going on here!" Devaney roared. "You act like this one's done and you're getting ready for next week. You can't quit when you get behind. You're playing for Nebraska!" The freshmen learned an important lesson in team pride, rallying and winning, 32–23.

It was a high-water period for college football, and in the preceding decade there had been two number one versus number two face-offs with extraordinary buildup (Notre Dame vs. Michigan State in 1966, Arkansas vs. Texas in 1969) that were fine games but failed to deliver in the "best ever" category. Neither of the teams in those two games had the explosive offensive talent that would take the field in Nebraska vs. Oklahoma.

The essence of the showdown boiled down to the Nebraska defense versus the Oklahoma offense. The Sooners led the nation as a team with 563 yards per game, with slightly more than 481 of those yards gained on the ground. Nebraska's defense allowed only 171 yards per game, and that, too, was tops in the nation. The Husker defense gave up only 70 yards on the ground in an average game. The most intriguing aspect of the matchup, and the most important element in any game, was scoring. Oklahoma averaged 45 points per game, while Nebraska begrudgingly gave up only 6 points per game.

"I don't think we could have projected the stuff we did as a defense in 1971," said Jim Anderson. "We had some good players, some quality athletes, and we played some really good fundamental defense and didn't make any mistakes. And we had enough good talent to make some big plays. A guy like [defensive end] Willie Harper could make a big play when we needed it. It just developed as we went along. And, as we went into the Big Eight season, we had some shutouts, three in a row, and I think finally it dawned on us that we were pretty good. And we needed every bit of confidence going into that game with Oklahoma, because, man, that was a showdown. They had awesome offensive power. I don't think we had any big preconceived ideas about our defense going into the season. It just kind of developed into something solid.

"I was just glad we were finally going to get a chance to play the game," said Anderson. "The hype was building up and everybody else in the country had finished playing and this game was on Thanksgiving. We'd been heading for a showdown for a while, and then the last week, man, you turn on Monday Night Football and there's Howard Cosell hyping the game. Here we were, kids in our twenties, watching Howard Cosell pumping the game up. That's all there was everywhere you looked—this game—and ABC only ran one game a week. There's fifty games on now, but then there was only one game a week. So, the hype was really intense and most of us were really glad we could finally go play the game. We didn't change anything at practice, it just happened to be a really big game. Just like you see any of the coaches today say on TV before big games: 'We didn't change anything.' They don't say that because they have nothing else to say. It's actually true."

In the gathering storm, the practice field was a refuge for some. "I can remember Coach Switzer talking about Nebraska during practice and saying he hoped they ran an overshift defense like they did the year before against us," said Leon Crosswhite. "When I say overshift, that means more guys on one side of the ball than the other. The wishbone is an even attack on both sides, so the defense has to be just as even. They didn't do it, and we were hoping for it. If they did they wouldn't have a chance against us, because you just can't do that against the wishbone. We lost 28–21 to them in 1970, but we'd have beaten them if we were more familiar with the offense. But give credit to the Nebraska coaches: They figured that out and didn't play an overshift in '71. The thing we were most worried about regarding Nebraska was their size and strength. We knew they were going to be tough to block.

"I'd never been a part of a game like that where the media came in on a Monday," said Crosswhite. "Coach Switzer asked us to go by at certain times and meet with the media. That was the first time for anything like that for anyone on those OU teams. That gets you a little more hyped up. You start to think, 'Hmm, just how big is this game?'"

Tom Brahaney, Oklahoma's star center, was reveling in the obscurity that goes with being an offensive lineman. "There may have been a lot of press there," said Brahaney, "but the offensive linemen sure didn't see them. Probably Jack and Greg did, but none of us did. It was just a normal week for us, just go punch the clock. We knew it was a big game. We'd seen [Nebraska] on film and, shoot, nobody had scored many points on them or ran the ball on them at all. Rich Glover was the best defensive lineman in the country at the time. They weren't sort of crazy physical like Missouri, who would attack you and use forearms and played what I call 'hold a spot and die' defense. Nebraska's guys were strong, but they were also great athletes.

"I was from Midland High School, in Midland, Texas, and I went to Oklahoma so I could play in big games," said Brahaney. "We were not very good at all at Midland. We only won three games my senior year, so I wanted to go somewhere that had a chance to win. I was recruited by everyone in the Southwest Conference, but I wasn't interested in going anywhere but Oklahoma.

"Our offensive line coach was Bill Michael," said Brahaney. "He was a teammate of Switzer's at Arkansas, a tough hard-nosed guy who always had a chaw of tobacco in his cheek. And he'd get down and spit that tobacco and say stuff like, 'You gotta whip his ass and drive him off the ball and stay with him,' and all that sort of stuff. Dean Unruh and I were real good friends on the field, and a little off it too. Dean was an excellent drive-blocker, I mean he really could line up and drive-block. Every once in a while he'd have a little trouble with pass protection. We didn't throw the ball that much so it wasn't really exposed, but if he knew he was the only guy who was going to block a guy on a pass, he'd always say to me, 'Hey, man, look back just in case, because I don't know what's going to happen.' But shoot, we only threw the ball four or five times a game.

"Every Thursday or Friday at the end of practice, I'd drop back as a quarterback and throw Jack Mildren a pass," said Brahaney. "That was about the extent of our passing attack."

Another Oklahoma player from Midland was defensive back Steve O'Shaughnessy.

"I had a good friend who was in my class, Steve Aycock, who played with me through high school and into OU and he had a big influence on me going to the University of Oklahoma. I was actually accepted and enrolled in classes at Notre Dame. I was all set to go there and I happened to be invited on a recruiting trip by Steve and once I saw what they had [at Oklahoma] and the fact that Jack Mildren and Johnny Harrison from Abilene Cooper were there, I changed my mind. It turned out four of us from the same class from the same high school district, which was a very strong one in the country, decided to all show up there at the same time and then we added a fifth guy, Tom Brahaney, who was a class behind us out of my high school as well. So it turned out there was five of us from the same district starting in that game. But those guys and specifically Steve on that recruiting trip changed my mind up there.

"There were so many players who came up to Oklahoma from Texas that we felt like we knew each other at least. Growing up in West Texas, football was one of four major sports, the others being basketball, track, and baseball. You didn't really have much to choose from other than those. You didn't have lacrosse, which I probably would have played if they'd had it, and you didn't have soccer then. West Texas being the well-known football area that it is, you found yourself in it if you were able to play.

"Emotionally speaking," said O'Shaughnessy, "the feeling on campus that week was incredible. The entire campus was on fire about the game. We'd walk to class and sign autographs. Everyone was encouraging us. Everybody was behind us. I'd never seen anything like that in my life. You're on top of the world. As my good friend Steve Aycock told me a few years ago, 'Nobody told us at that time it was going to be all downhill from there.' When you're young and the talk of the university it's like having the biggest fan club of all time. It was amazing when you were twenty-one years old, the way the public backed us and how you just really felt you were at the pinnacle of your life at the time and it turns out that you were.

"During our practices that week we did the same stuff we did all the time," said O'Shaughnessy. "We did a lot of running all year long for conditioning, because that's what we had to do during the game. And a lot of skill-type drills, interception-type drills, covering-type drills because we played man-to-man coverage. Other than that we focused on the task at hand every given week, which is who we were going to play and what they did and how to prevent it. In college, once you get to that level of play, it's really concentrating on who your opponent is that week more than anything else. It may have been a bit more intense because of the hoopla surrounding the week. The press was bothering us all week, and there was a real electric feeling all week on the practice field, off the practice field, in class, just walking around. The feeling was very, very unusual, but the actual preparation was very similar to any week.

"The members of our coaching staff turned out to be pretty famous later in life. Jimmy Johnson went on to the Miami Dolphins and the Dallas Cowboys, and Barry Switzer and nearly everyone else all became head coaches at major colleges, with the pros, or both. Looking back, at the time those guys were all in their late twenties. They were young kids, but they were older to us of course. They were accomplished coaches and we had a great amount of respect for them because of their knowledge base, their intelligence, and how they taught us. I think Jimmy Johnson had the best attitude of any coach on the field—the practice field at least. He was always smiling, always laughing. My coach, Jimmy Dickey, who ended up as the head coach of Kansas State, was serious, extremely knowledgeable, and a tremendous teacher. The reason they were all successful then was the consistency of how they prepared us every week.

"As part of our preparation for games in Norman they would put us on a bus on Friday afternoon after a quick warm-up on the field—we wouldn't really practice—and take us into Oklahoma City and put us up at a hotel. For the Nebraska game we would have done that Wednesday. That's what they did every week. Once there, they didn't give you a lot of time to mess around. We had a team meeting here and there, we had dinner, we'd go to a movie, you'd go back to your room and go to bed. I think it was good that they didn't give us a lot of time to dwell on it, although the atmosphere was very nervous, at least it was for me. Any diversion we could get, like a movie, was welcome. I was pretty nervous the night before the game.

"I don't recall having any trouble sleeping," said O'Shaughnessy, "but the next morning, that nervousness started to build again on the bus trip back to Norman. As you're approaching kickoff—thirty minutes, ten minutes—and you know it's inevitable that you have to go out there and they're going to blow that whistle, that's when you really get the butterflies building up."

For Oklahoma kicker John Carroll, the big-game feeling around Oklahoma was something he was very familiar with, and the night before the Nebraska game was routine. "I'd been around OU football all my life and I bled crimson and cream," said Carroll. "My dad, Bill, was the track coach at OU from 1955 to 1968. I'd grown up in Norman, been through the Wilkinson years and the Mackenzie era. I'd just been around it and I liked playing it. I had fun doing it. I was player of the year in Oklahoma in high school basketball. It was either go to Kansas and play basketball for Ted Owens or play football at OU. My decision was pretty easy.

"The night before the Nebraska game was really a normal night. We ate lunch at the dorm, then we got on our buses to go to Oklahoma City to spend the night before the game. Went to a movie, I think it was *Patton* or the one with Burt Reynolds when he's in prison, *The Longest Yard*. We came back after, got our hot chocolate and Hershey bars, and had a team meeting and went upstairs and went to bed. It was pretty normal. I think that's what they tried to do, make it a normal deal."

To Sooner sophomore defensive lineman Lucious Selmon, the difference in the week of the Nebraska game was noticeable. "Being as young as I was, it was a brand-new experience for me. Of course, that was the first year in a while they'd had a real good year there. We had great players on both sides of the ball. A lot of super, super athletes. And the student body was really behind us, the whole city was. And anywhere you went, people were always praising us and wishing us luck. I had no idea of the increased magnitude of the game with Nebraska. It didn't hit me until the week of the game. I had no comprehension of how big that game was. I knew people were saying that it was probably going to determine who the national champion was going to be, and the conference champion, and everywhere you went you saw banners and signs. I could tell there was a difference in the preparation of the older players, because I remember there was an upperclassman running scout team; he was an offensive guard named Ron Stacy. And I'll tell you what, he prepared me real good for that game. He was a big guy and knocked the heck out of me all week long and got me ready. The upperclassmen knew what it was all about, and I was only just gaining a grasp of it, not as clear as they had.

"I remember the Wednesday afternoon before the Nebraska game, Jimmy Johnson called us in to talk," said Selmon. "That was normal; he did that every week. But instead of talking to us all together he talked to us one at a time. And he told us about the importance of the game, and to make sure we carried out our assignments. And I remember saying to myself, 'This is a little bit different; we've never done this before.' The day that I went in to visit with Coach Johnson I wasn't feeling well. I had a fever, and I know I wasn't sick. I was so nervous I gave myself a fever."

Like their counterparts at Oklahoma, Nebraska's veteran players experienced a new, and strange, anxiety brought on by the impending game. "For some reason, we brought our own food supply with us to Oklahoma City," said safety Bill Kosch. At the very least, Nebraska wanted the assurance that they wouldn't lose the game to an unexpected case of food poisoning.

ELEVEN

Oft expectation fails, and most oft there
Where most it promises; and oft it hits
Where hope is coldest and despair most fits.

—*All's Well That Ends Well,* by William Shakespeare

LUCIOUS SELMON WAS JUST A SOPHOMORE, BUT BY midway through the season he'd worked his way into Oklahoma's starting lineup as a defensive tackle. He was widely considered by his teammates and coaches to be the strongest player on the Sooner team. "Yes," said Selmon nearly thirty-five years later, "I had gained that distinction. It was just God-given strength. We grew up in a small town in southeast Oklahoma called Eufaula, and you got strong from the manual labor and working out in the country. We didn't have modern farm equipment back then. We plowed the fields with mules. And we didn't have chainsaws—we chopped big trees down with an ax. We dug postholes, worked with livestock, lifted hogs, wrassled steer. Steer wrasslin' was a sport for some people, but for us it was a job. And we did that with quite a bit of ease. Our dad used to say to us, 'I want you boys to go out there and catch that steer, but take it easy on him. Don't break his neck.'

"When I was a freshman at Oklahoma," said Selmon, "a Fellowship of Christian Athletes weight lifter came to the school, and was demonstrating how to lift weights. I gave it a try and lifted more weight than he did and I didn't have a belt on."

The change from life on the farm in Eufaula to university life was "a major transition for me," said Selmon. "I came from a country where we still had outdoor bathrooms and no running water in the house. All of the sudden I'm living in a nice dormitory, and the student body was ten times larger than the population of my whole town. One class was bigger than that whole student body of my high school."

Two years earlier, Selmon had almost headed for Colorado. "I was a fullback in high school, and thought I would be the next Jim Brown or something of that nature. I was recruited by OU and all the other schools in the state. I really fell in love with the University of Colorado. The head coach there at the time was Eddie Crowder, who was a graduate and who had played at OU, and my folks really enjoyed Coach Crowder.

"And at that time," said Selmon, "coaches could take you out to dinner, lunch, and all that stuff, and that was a big deal to me, being raised as we were. We didn't get meat at every meal and all that. So that was a wonderful time of the year for me when I was being recruited. One school would catch up with me at lunchtime and I'd get a nice steak dinner. Then dinnertime would come around and I'd get another nice steak dinner. As long as they were coming, I was eating it. Eddie Crowder did a great job recruiting me, and I thought about signing a letter of intent to go there.

"Larry Lacewell from Oklahoma was recruiting me, too, but I had verbally committed to Eddie Crowder right in our home," said Selmon. "Right after he left, Coach Lacewell showed up and he turned me around, mostly because my mother made the statement that she would like to see me stay close to home rather than go to Colorado. That was the changing deal in the whole thing. If that statement hadn't been made, I would have gone to Colorado. And I made the phone call and told Coach Crowder that I'd decided to stay close to home, and that was the only way that he wasn't able to convince me that Colorado was a better choice from me. He couldn't tell me the distance from Colorado was shorter to my home, and that my folks would have an easier time of things getting to see me play. He was truthful enough to say he couldn't overcome that one, and wished me luck."

Now, on Thanksgiving morning, the still relatively green Selmon woke up to find himself smack in the middle of something with which he was totally unfamiliar. "Normally we had a police escort down to Norman from the hotel in Oklahoma City," said Selmon, "and normally we would make that trip pretty easily. But the traffic was unbelievable. I had never seen traffic like it in all my life. So many cars and so many people trying to get down to a game that early in the day. And the well-wishers were really, really thick at the gate where the bus pulled up for us to go into the stadium. I thought there were a lot of them when we played Texas, but there was so many people it was just unbelievable. It was a sea of red— everybody had red on. Just so many people. They had little barricades to make a passage for us, but there was no tunnel or anything. We had to get off the bus and walk through the people. You had all kinds of cheers, and people patting you on the back. Mark Driscoll was a senior, and when he exited the bus just in front of me and saw all the people, he looked over his shoulder at me and said, 'God, this is a *big* ballgame.'"

The immediate pregame routine was nearly the same for all football teams. After arriving at the stadium, the players would put on their uniforms without the shoulder pads, then sit around waiting for their position coaches to order them onto the field to go through warm-ups. An hour before kickoff, the field became a blur of synchronized activity, with each team assigned an L-shaped chunk of the field, including one full end zone, for warm-up drills. Kickoffs and punts were boomed, caught at the opposite end of the field, and the balls relayed back to the kickers. Passes floated to receivers, handoffs were practiced for the millionth time. Eyes stole glances at the opposition, in many cases seeing them in person for the first time and bringing to mind the words of Dwight Eisenhower that "your opponent always seems fourteen feet tall." Then the teams returned to the dressing room to gather themselves before bursting onto the field immediately preceding the kickoff.

"Normally back then, when we were preparing for a game, we'd all have programs of the opposing team in our lockers," said Selmon. "During that quiet time, I went through my program and looked at the defensive players first. I looked at Rich Glover and Larry Jacobson. Then I flipped over and looked at Jerry Tagge, and Rodgers, and Jeff Kinney, all these guys I'd heard of, these great players. I had to psyche myself into knowing they were the same as me. They have football pants on and football pads on, and they're going to try to hit me and I'm going to do my best to try to hit them.

"When we took the field for warm-ups," said Selmon, "we had our ritual of running back and forth across the end zone, and as I was running, I saw Jeff Kinney take a handoff from Tagge. Now, I'd heard about something called tunnel vision, and I decided I would watch Kinney and try to tunnel-vision him, and make him look small. And I think I was successful doing that.

"Then I saw Johnny Rodgers catching punts," said Selmon, "and when he took off running, it looked like he was floating on air. He was unbelievably quick. You couldn't tunnel-vision a guy like that. You'd never get him in the tunnel. That image of him stayed in my mind, and the next time I saw the guy catch a punt, it was for real, and he still looked like he was floating on air and was even quicker."

When the team returned to the locker room prior to kickoff, "there wasn't a lot of joking or anything when we went inside the dressing room," said Selmon. "Everyone got settled and taped up, then everyone was putting the pads on. A lot of teams we'd played that year, we just ran through them. Our offense seemed like they scored almost every time they took the field. But this time, I'm a sophomore in there with all these upperclassmen, and I noticed an eerie quiet in the dressing room. Nobody was saying much of anything. Guys had big wads of gum, that this little guy standing near the gate always gave us, and everybody was nervously chewing the gum. I'd never witnessed that kind of quiet before. And it stayed that way until Coach Fairbanks came in and addressed us.

"Coach Fairbanks was one of these kind of low, soft-talking

type of guys," said Selmon, "but you could read his expressions. The players used to talk about his evil eye, and his expressions said more than his words, but I remember his words from that day. I'll never forget them."

"You came to the University of Oklahoma to play in these types of games," Fairbanks told his team. "Now, if you want to win the biggest ballgame that most of us will ever play in our life, well, here's your opportunity. Let's make the best of it."

Selmon looked around and thought to himself, "*Damn*, this *is* big."

In gusty winds and under overcast skies, with temperatures in the mid-fifties, the ball was kicked off at 1:50 Central Standard Time. The Huskers wore their white road jerseys and red pants. Oklahoma, wearing their crimson shirts, was on the receiving end of the kick, but Mildren and the wishbone didn't produce any fireworks on the first possession. The only thing of note that happened was that Sooner fullback Leon Crosswhite dinged his knee, and briefly left the game, replaced by Tim Welch. "I got hurt the first running play of the game," said Crosswhite. "I got stood up on the line, and Joe Blahak came in full speed and hit the inside of my knee with his helmet."

With just 3:32 elapsed in the game, Joe Wylie dropped back to punt for the Sooners, and hit a nose-diving knuckleball that seemed unlikely to be returned. It was fielded by Johnny Rodgers at the Nebraska twenty-eight-yard line. Within a few seconds, Rodgers was in the Oklahoma end zone for the game's first score.

The first player down the field on coverage was Greg Pruitt. "Johnny and I were friends," said Pruitt. "We used to have phone conversations, and we'd talk noise to each other about who was the better player and who was going to do this or that in a game. I would have a good game and call him and say, 'I scored so many touchdowns; how'd you do?' That personal relationship led to me making a big mistake on that punt. When you cover a punt return of an explosive player, you always break down. You never take a shot at him. You just slow him down, make sure you have help, and then attack him. I didn't do that, because I wanted to brag to him the next week about how I slammed him. I was the first guy down on that punt return, and I got my hands on him, but I couldn't hold him. And I held him just enough for three guys to miss him. Of course, one of them got clipped."

"That return was designed to go to the right," said Fairbanks years later, "and Rodgers ran to the left after spinning away from Greg's tackle, and made a marvelous individual effort to score. I don't know anything about blown calls. I would never claim that. If Greg had made that tackle, though, he might have been playing defense the rest of his career."

Rodgers's punt return was such a feast for the eyes that it's considered one of the great plays in college football history. As Nebraska radio play-by-play man Lyell Bremser called it, "Holy moly. Man, woman, and child did that put 'em in the aisles." Rodgers vividly recalled the play: "Pruitt didn't break down and I was able to shake him. He grabbed and pulled me, but I got loose, caught my balance, and broke to my right. Another man crossed my face, forcing me to the middle of the field and I was running directly toward the referee. He tried to get out of my way and I broke left toward the sideline and got a great block, and was gone. I went to the sidelines afterward and vomited."

The "great block" was thrown by Joe Blahak, and, in the minds of Sooner fans, was clearly an illegal block in the back. "I'm the guy everyone says got clipped on the Johnny Rodgers return," said Jon Harrison. "I like to tell people I was just to get them going, but I really wasn't.

"Back then, you could only substitute two players on a play," said Harrison. "That was a rule. Not too many people remember that rule about only two guys could come off. When you took the field at the change of possession, anybody could go in the game, but on any other play you could only substitute two people at one time. I was only 160 pounds and I was the tight end sometimes on extra points. So all the offensive linemen were covering on that punt, and so back then you could have big plays because those guys don't ever really work on tackling. I had outside contain on the right, and I sort of forced him back into the middle and then got pushed out of bounds. Then I turned around and ran down the sideline and he got cornered and came back toward me, and I was just about to reach for him and I got blocked. It was on the side, and you could block below the waist back then."

Dean Unruh was also downfield on the play. "A lot of guys missed him, me included," said Unruh years later while laughing. "For about five years after that, a buddy of mine sent me a Christmas card with the photo sequence of the punt return from *Sports Illustrated*. I'm in one of them, of course. They didn't let me forget. Every once in a while I'll be sitting somewhere and I'll look up at the televison and there's Johnny Rodgers scoring and me missing him. I can't get away from that. Once I was with the guy who used to send me the Christmas card, we looked up and saw the play on TV and he said, 'Yep, you still missed him.'"

"Needless to say," said Unruh, "we only worked on punt coverage ten thousand times that week to make sure that wouldn't happen. But Johnny was a great player, and great players make great plays."

Rodgers's return was a big play, but it was too early in the game to be considered a turning point. "It did very little to us emotionally," said Unruh. "It was something we didn't want to let happen, and I'm as much at fault as anyone else because I missed him. I was one of the guys that missed the tackle, but you can't dwell on that. You know, you gotta go play. In general, my mind-set was, we have the whole game left, let's just go play. And I don't think I ever played any different ahead or behind. That never entered my mind. I just went out and played."

"It didn't faze us," said Crosswhite. "I should have been on the punt coverage team. Usually I was the fullback on punts, but my backup was in there. Timmy Welch hadn't gotten to play that much and had never played defense in high school.

"Of course," said Crosswhite with a chuckle, "I always felt like if I was in there, I would have got Rodgers."

"I don't even think I saw the whole play on the sidelines," said Jack Mildren. "I've seen it a gazillion times since. At the time, I probably just said, 'Oh hell, I can't believe that.' But it was just something we needed to overcome.

"As I reflect on it," said Mildren, "it was a pretty impressive statement for a team on the road. Not a bad way to go get an easy one, particularly for a team that tended to grind them out. They were a powerful football team. That was the one play that nobody planned on."

The score was 7–0 in Nebraska's favor, but Mildren was about to get the Sooners moving.

On the possession following Rodgers's touchdown run, Oklahoma drove the ball all the way down to the Cornhusker thirteen-yard line before the Blackshirts held their ground. John Carroll, who grew up within shouting distance of Owen Field, put the Sooners on the board with a 30-yard field goal. With 5:57 left in the first quarter, the score was 7–3.

The importance of the Sooners' initial scoring drive went far beyond the three points it produced, however. It was *how* Oklahoma got into scoring position that was most curious, and it provided the first major clue to how the game would unfold. The key play on the drive was not a Pruitt dash or a Wylie scamper. Nor was it a Crosswhite jailbreak up the middle, or a Mildren keeper. It was a 32-yard pass to Jon Harrison, Mildren's old battery mate from Abilene Cooper, and with that connection, the chink in the armor of the mighty Blackshirts was revealed.

Not a soul in the stands or a single person watching on television around the world noticed, but in preparation for the game Nebraska had made a strategic shift in the deployment of two veteran secondary players, junior Joe Blahak and senior Bill Kosch. The two had been best friends since high school.

"I went to a small Catholic high school in Columbus, Nebraska, about a hundred miles west of Omaha," said Bill Kosch. "My senior year I think we had thirty-three guys on the football team, including freshmen. But we ended up being state champ of the smaller schools. We were more like a track team in shoulder pads. One of my teammates was Joe Blahak, who was a year behind me. I was a defensive back and halfback, and Joe was the other halfback and other cornerback. Joe was a fantastic track man. He had a step on me. He was 100- and 200-meter champion, and low hurdler. I ran high and low hurdles. We both did the long jump and triple jump. Joe could pole-vault and I did the shot and discus. We were best friends off the field, still are to this day.

"There I was," said Kosch, "at this small school, not thinking I was anything special, not even necessarily thinking about college. People were telling me, 'You'll end up going to some college,' and all I could think was, 'Well, you have to be pretty good to get a scholarship.' I got three letters: one from the Air Force Academy because my coach put in for me, and I wasn't interested in going in the air force. I got a letter from Notre Dame and a letter from Nebraska. That was it. As far as Notre Dame, I just wasn't interested. I grew up thinking about the Cornhuskers. I listened to the games, but I'd never attended one. Going down to Lincoln in 1967, that was a big drive. It was almost 100 miles. You just didn't do things like that. Taking a 500-mile trip once a year was a family vacation. Today it's a weekend trip.

"Cletus Fischer came down and talked to me after football season, during a basketball practice. We went back in the coaches' offices, and he asked me how fast I was. I got a letter around January asking me if I'd accept a full scholarship to the university. On signing day, Don Bryant [Nebraska's sports information director] came to my house, and my dad and my mother and I were sitting at the kitchen table, and it was just a matter of a few pen strokes and I was a Cornhusker. My dad didn't have any questions about it and my mom was worried about whether they had washing machines at the school.

"Joe didn't need any help from me once he got to Nebraska," said Kosch. "He stood on his own merits. He was a special athlete. I became a starter my junior year, 1970, and Joe started the same year as a sophomore. We were a very veteran secondary in 1971.

"Not many people know they decided to switch us around for the Oklahoma game," said Kosch, whose regular position was safety. Blahak was a cornerback. "It's like any other sport: You see the result but you don't know all the integrated moves that go into making something work or what made it fail. It [the change] was a total surprise to me. We worked on it for a week in practice, but I never felt comfortable with it. It's not like I never covered anybody one-on-one. I would practice doing the out coverages, and one-on-ones and deep breaks along with the corners all the time, but I had a stance and a depth that I liked to play at. I was comfortable at six yards off the receiver and one yard out [toward the sideline shoulder of the receiver]. That way I took away the outside throw and knew if I was going to get beat it would be on the inside, and that's where the other ten guys on your team are. But for the Oklahoma game, they wanted me to play a whole new technique—ten yards off the receiver and head up on him. And I just . . . I didn't believe in it, but that's what they wanted me to do, so I tried.

"The theory on the whole coverage," said Kosch, "was that they didn't want to get beat deep so they put me deep to start with. And Mildren was not what you would call a skilled drop-back passer. They only threw the ball four or five times a game. The theory was that when they did try to surprise you it would be a deep ball straight down the field, and since I would be ten yards ahead of the receiver, I'd have it covered. And when Mildren threw the ball it wasn't going to be a precision throw, it was just going to be in the general area, so I'd have as good a chance at getting it as the receiver. That was the theory, at least."

"In fairness to Bill [Kosch], what we did wasn't at all fair to him," said Monte Kiffin nearly thirty-five years later. "We had to stop the run, of course. The whole deal back in those days was stopping the wishbone and Oklahoma was the best at it. When

Jack Mildren got up under center, there was nobody better at running an option attack. And we just *had* to stop Greg Pruitt.

"Joe Blahak was an excellent, excellent tackler," said Kiffin, "and so we moved him from the cornerback position to what we call putting the ninth guy in the box. We more or less had him manned up on Greg Pruitt. He eyeballed and mirrored Greg Pruitt all day. And we really did a good job on Pruitt, but we gave up something on the pass defense because Blahak was also a very good cover corner. The thing that threw us off was that we never imagined Mildren would be able to throw the ball that well, you know. We had ten people up playing the run and we had single coverage on the outside receiver."

"I was a little nervous before the game because I wasn't in my own position," said Kosch. "I really was on an island. It was like two different games were being played at the same time. One game of ten-on-ten and the other was one-on-one. It was like two different setups. I'm sure Jon [Harrison] loved it."

TWELVE

Canst thou draw out leviathan with a hook?

—Job 41:1

THE PLAN THAT LEFT NEBRASKA'S BILL KOSCH IN THE wilderness paid dividends late in the first quarter. "What was hard about the wishbone is that Mildren was so good at the option that it was hard to get your scout team to be able to run it in practice," said Monte Kiffin. "Oklahoma had so much speed in those days, and we couldn't give our defense a good look [in practice] because whatever speed it was it wasn't going to be game speed.

"The biggest thing we did was try to take the pitch away from Oklahoma," said Kiffin. "We put our defensive ends upfield on the pitch man, because we didn't want to give them the pitch. We wanted to make Mildren keep the ball. If someone was going to beat us running the ball, we wanted it to be Mildren, because the pitch was where they got so many of their big plays. You pitch the ball out to Wylie or Pruitt and it's trouble. We moved the tackles and the ends out some, probably about two feet wider. Blahak spied Pruitt on just about every play, more or less mirrored him. I remember it like it was yesterday. Number 30, Greg Pruitt, that's a guy that kept you up at night."

The Blackshirts were swarming all over the Sooner rushing attack as the final seconds ticked off the first quarter and Joe Blahak put the wood to Pruitt, who fumbled. Jim Anderson recovered the ball near midfield. Anderson was lurking near the line of scrimmage, too, thanks to another defensive wrinkle installed by Kiffin.

"I was playing over the tight end, Albert Chandler," said Anderson. "My role was to read whether it was run or pass based on what he did. I was up really much tighter than I normally would have been. I was creeping up—instead of being six, seven yards off like you would off a wide receiver, or five or six yards like a normal tight end, I was up there four to five yards off looking for a real quick key to support on either Mildren or Pruitt depending on what defense had been called. Based on the close game we had with them the year prior, we realized how quick you have to react to this thing. That goes back to my point of how tight I was play-ing Chandler. I had to make an instant read. I was playing really aggressively, reading instantly, and reacting on what I needed to do. So I was putting myself under a lot of pressure by playing that tight. If he blocked in any way I was going to support the run quickly. If he released then I was the only one on him; and I had to cover him one-on-one. If he blocked, I supported. If he released, I went with him.

"We could do that because the [offensive] formation basically stayed the same," said Anderson. "It's not like nowadays where teams come out in a million different formations. The formations stayed pretty consistent. So, I played over the tight end every time they lined up.

"[The coaches] took Joe [Blahak], who was our fastest guy, and they put him in the middle to support the run either way and thought that was the most important thing. Joe was our quickest, fastest guy and a big hitter. Everyone's role was a little bit different than normal."

After the fumble, Tagge and the Cornhusker offense took over at their own forty-six-yard line and efficiently moved the ball down the field, using a little more than four minutes. With 11:08 left in the first half, Jeff Kinney hammered the ball into the end zone from a yard out, and Nebraska led 14–3.

"When you played the wishbone you had to make sure you accounted for it all," said Monte Kiffin, "the dive and the quarterback and the pitch. Our players were very good students of the game, and we really understood their blocking schemes. You had to because a defense could just get shell-shocked if that thing got going." Kiffin's strategy had effectively removed Pruitt from Oklahoma's early drives, and the Blackshirts seemed poised to completely choke off the Sooner rushing attack.

"One thing Kiffin had us do," said Larry Jacobson, "was when they would fake to the fullback, it was the defensive tackles' responsibility to grab the fullback every time he came at us so he couldn't get downfield to block the linebacker. Then the linebackers could flow outside. Whether he [Leon Crosswhite] had the ball or not, we knocked him down so he couldn't get downfield to block the linebackers. That was a little different."

"It wasn't a matter of them keying on Greg [Pruitt] so much," said Fairbanks. "It was a matter of how they allowed their inside linebackers to flow to the outside. And they did it better than anybody we'd seen prior to that team."

While that was all true, even a novice fan in the cheap seats could see that the person doing the most direct damage to the Oklahoma offense was the 6' 1", 234-pound Cornhusker nose guard, Rich Glover. "Richie Glover was the nose tackle in our defense," said Monte Kiffin, "and pretty early in the game Coach Devaney came over—and he very seldom did this, he let the coordinators do most of the coaching—and called the whole defense together. He said, 'Richie Glover has tackled the fullback, the quarterback, and the pitch man. What are the rest of you doing out there?' That got everyone's attention. But Richie really was making a lot of plays that day."

"Rich Glover was the quietest guy on our team," said Jim Anderson. "He let his play do the talking."

It was hardly the toughest game of Glover's football life. He'd played his high school football at Snyder High in Jersey City, New

Jersey, where in one memorable game his team upset rival Lincoln High, the top-ranked team in the state. "We had them beat," Glover said, "and there wasn't much time left. Our cornerback broke up a play and their guy flipped him over his back and started a fight. People ran onto the field from all over the place. I was clear on the other side of the field, and by the time I got there all I could do was jump on the big pile of people." Fifty mounted police officers finally rode onto the field to disperse the mob. On another occasion, Glover's high school coach told his team to bring trash-can lids on the bus to an away game, just in case they won and the opposition fans pelted the windows of the bus with rocks.

Glover lined up across from Sooner All-American center Tom Brahaney on every play. Brahaney had an inch on Glover, but otherwise the two were fairly comparable in size. Nevertheless, it was a mismatch. "Glover just ate him alive," said Jacobson. "He was so quick that he could get around the center and catch the option from the side. If he didn't get 'em, I got 'em, and sometimes we got 'em together." By day's end, Glover was in on 22 tackles, and Jacobson on 14.

"Tom Brahaney was a wonderful player," said Fairbanks, "and so was Glover. You have to go into a game thinking that if we went purely one-on-one they would both end up winning their share of the battles. Glover was a guy who was good enough to disrupt another team's offense all by himself."

"Glover lined up on my nose," said Brahaney years later. "He had a great game, but he really made a lot of tackles on the outside with his pursuit. I'd try to block him on one side and he'd come around the back side and run to the sidelines. Our option didn't work at all. Coach Switzer told me Rich would overplay one side. Like if we were going to run to our right, say, a fullback handoff to the right, Rich would kind of play across your head real fast. So if the play was going right, for instance, Switzer told me to put my head on the left side to give him a false read so he'd play across my head. A false-influence block you might call that.

"Now, they were in their predetermined defense where they were going to take one side or the other no matter what," said Brahaney, "so it didn't matter where your head went because they were going there anyway. I got killed right off the bat. Switzer claims he never told me that, but he did. I remember looking up at the press box, where he was during the game, and shaking my head and thinking, 'I'm not going to do that anymore.' The couple times I tried it, Glover did make plays all by himself."

"We understood that we were playing against great players who were just as capable of making plays as we were," said Jack Mildren. "We knew it wouldn't be perfect. There would be some struggles, and the key was to limit them to physical struggles and not mental struggles. The advantage of the wishbone, theoretically, is that you ought to be able to take advantage of what people do; you don't have to guess. Not that every play was pure. Nebraska lined up in a five technique [five linemen], and the five techniques counted on beating you with players.

"People did so many things against us that we couldn't anticipate they would focus on shutting down Pruitt," said Mildren. "On the other hand, Texas had played us like that—gotten people wide to prevent the pitch—but Greg'd had some success against them. Texas just didn't have Nebraska players. We were playing on the theory that once the ball was snapped we'd react to what they were doing. We had to limit mental mistakes and win what physical wars we could. If they were going to do something on the corner, we'd never find out until we go line up because everyone tries to do something their own way."

Perhaps, thought Switzer and Galen Hall, up in the press box looking at the action, if they couldn't run away from Glover, they could use his speed to their advantage. And if Nebraska wanted to take away the outside, Oklahoma would hit 'em on the inside. "All of our blocking schemes didn't require one-on-one blocking," said Fairbanks. "We thought some of the blocking schemes we used on the misdirection-counter plays up inside took advantage of Glover's quickness and speed to react in one direction and we ran the ball in another direction, away from that. That helped us—and it helped Brahaney to be successful one-on-one."

"On any counter you take a step or two in the opposite direction of where you're going to really go," said Leon Crosswhite. "You're trying to get the defensive linemen and linebackers to take a wrong step, to plant their foot to go the wrong way. Then we counter right back. And in the wishbone the counter happens quicker than any other offense I know of. You can counter so fast—of course, by then they're running so fast to the end to try to stop you if you've had any success on the outside—that's where the counters come in. And it only takes one step for it to be effective. And it helps guys like me get a better angle on the block."

Unbowed by the early pressure, Mildren ran the counter plays right into the heart of the Nebraska defense, keeping the ball himself six times for 43 yards. Grinding out yards instead of swallowing them up in huge gulps, the Sooners drove 80 yards for a touchdown. After faking the dive to Crosswhite, Mildren took the ball in for the score from the two-yard line. He ran wide and crossed into the end zone untouched. The score was 14–10.

"We ran the ball against them real well up the middle," said Brahaney. "A lot of those runs were counter plays. I think they had predetermined that they were going to go a particular way. So if you caught them on a step, especially on a quarterback counter, Jack would take a step one way and then just get right in behind me and pick up 10 yards or so."

"They put in a new counter play and we weren't ready for the blocking scheme on what we referred to as counter-dive option," said Kiffin. "They ran a counter-dive option and put in a new blocking scheme we hadn't seen, and they really did a good job with that. Galen Hall and those guys did a good job coming up with that, and it threw us off. Before they always blocked with the tight end, but now they released the tight end, which they had not shown before. They released the tight end downfield on Jimmy Anderson, and that was something they hadn't shown before on film, and that let Mildren get some yards. Jimmy Anderson had to cover the tight end for the pass. Had the tight end been blocking, Jimmy Anderson would have had the quarterback. They attacked what we were doing right away."

They'd never left it, of course, but if there had been any doubters, the Sooners had shown they were back in the fight.

There were just fifty-five seconds left in the first half when Oklahoma took over on its own twenty-two-yard line. Up in the press box, Barry Switzer and Galen Hall sent down word that rather than risk a turnover, Mildren should run out the clock. The two coaches took off their headsets and headed for the elevator that led down to the locker rooms. After two running plays, Mildren and Jon Harrison had a quick exchange in the huddle.

"I didn't know going into the game they were going to move Kosch," said Harrison. "I remember coming out after the first series of the game and the coaches telling me that this is probably what they were going to be doing the rest of the game. They are going to try to stop us running and we probably would have to pass some. I can't remember that it threw me at all, just remember thinking I was going to be man-on-man.

"I didn't know a lot about Kosch before going into the game," said Harrison. "They ran a lot of zone and that day they played man-to-man. It didn't surprise me because we were a running attack. It's almost like playing with ten people on each team. He'd be on me and I'd be on him and everybody else would be playing the run. We'd had some other teams do that, but they couldn't stop us running the ball, so we really didn't have to pass. But Nebraska had the number one defense in the country, and we weren't able to run the ball as well as we had on most people.

"We had some routes we thought could work against man-to-man," said Harrison. "Since we didn't throw the ball very much we just ran simple patterns—flags and posts were about the only things we ran. The hope was that if we ever needed one, I could just outrun the defender. I wasn't a great open-field runner, but my straight speed was pretty good and I had good hands.

"I knew the man routes that we could run would probably work," said Harrison. "Blahak was playing safety, and he was really just playing Jack. He'd go whichever way the ball went."

"Based on what Jon told me, we both thought he could beat Billy Kosch from the first time he went out there," said Jack Mildren. "Jon caught a corner route on the first or second series going north, and it was easy. It wasn't the best pass I ever threw, but it was completed and we kicked a field goal and we just kind of looked at each other after that."

"And of course," said Kosch, "we were starting to stuff the run, so they started to throw the ball more than normal."

"I think it helped a lot that Jack and I grew up together and had thrown so many passes together," said Harrison. "So, when we got the ball right before half, Jack asked me what pass I wanted to run and I ran a post and got the ball down to about the Nebraska twenty-five."

"I had that pass covered and I was two steps ahead of him," said Kosch. "I just couldn't find the ball. It was underthrown a little bit. And then Harrison turned around, and by the time I turned around the ball was falling into his hands, and Blahak was chasing him. Joe went to stick [Harrison] but he hit me and popped my helmet off. Joe was a hitter, and my helmet popped right off my head. I think I was looking for my helmet when they ran the next play."

Back in the huddle, Mildren again asked Harrison what pattern he wanted. "I ran a flag route on the other side," said Harrison.

"And again," said Kosch, "here it came. Christ, I can't deny him any route because they want me head-up, and he runs a post corner. So I dip in and as soon as I dip in he dips out, and he gets a step on me. And Mildren placed the ball in there perfectly. Bang! Touchdown. Some quarterbacks are passers, some are throwers. Jack was a grenade thrower. From all the films I watched on him, he just kind of put the ball in the area. That day, Jack was perfect.

He rose to the challenge. If I had to pick another guy to be my leader off some other team we played, I'd pick Jack. He was a competitor and tough and smart. Everything you want."

"In the five football seasons I played with Jon Harrison—three in high school and two in college—I can count his drops on one hand," said Mildren. "He didn't drop the ball."

In just four plays, two of them passes, Oklahoma had covered 78 yards and scored against the number one defense in the land. The clock showed five seconds when Harrison put the Sooners ahead for the first time in the game, 17–14.

"The score right before the half was big for us, because we got ahead," said Mildren. "Maybe it shouldn't have happened, but it did. We didn't have time to do anything, and all of the sudden, we have the lead and it's halftime. The fans were going nuts."

It was the first time the entire season that Nebraska trailed in a game.

"We had been ahead there for a while," said Jim Anderson, "and that touchdown was kind of devastating. I think we were a little shook up there. We just had to regroup and refocus and keep at it. We just had to have faith that we were going to do it."

"We were the number one and two teams all year, and we knew it was coming down to whether our defense could stop their offense, or at least slow it down," said Larry Jacobson. "Looking back on it, what was so crazy and so stupid, was they took one of our safeties and put him man-to-man on Jon Harrison. I mean, [Kosch] hadn't played there since in junior high. We stopped the run, but shit, they just kept throwing the damn ball on us. It was just crazy."

THIRTEEN

The guts carry the feet, not the feet the guts.

—Cervantes, *Don Quixote de la Mancha*

NEBRASKA WAS FORCED TO FACE SOME HARSH FACTS at halftime. The Blackshirts had allowed Oklahoma to keep the ball for 18:51 of the first thirty minutes of play. Oklahoma had piled up 311 yards to Nebraska's anemic 91 yards. Oklahoma had 14 first downs, Nebraska had managed just 5. The Huskers had taken away Oklahoma's bread-and-butter big play—the pitch at the corner—but in doing so exposed themselves.

"They were stunned when that [touchdown] happened in the final minute," said Nebraska defensive backfield coach Warren Powers. "You could see it on their faces."

Bill Kosch had been handed an extraordinarily difficult assignment. He was an All–Big Eight selection the previous year at safety, but now he felt like a rookie cornerback. "Johnny Harrison was working against a guy who was a true freshman that day. I spent my whole career starting as a safety, and in the blink of an eye I was a freshman again. It was like taking a center and trying to make a forward out of him. He knows what a basketball looks like, and he knows how to dribble and shoot, but he's out of position. It's all different. I never felt comfortable standing out there."

Since the Huskers were a team of action rather than talk, the most Kosch got at halftime was quiet empathy. His teammates knew that what had been asked of him bordered on the impossible. "I probably just told Bill to hang in there," said Jim Anderson. "I didn't give him any great words of wisdom."

Kosch decided to ask for some help. "At halftime I went over to the coach [Powers] and said, 'Let me play him six [yards] off. Let me get in the feel of this,'" said Kosch.

"No, we don't want you up there," came the response. "We want you to stay deep."

"Let me come up and chuck him a couple of times and rattle his head," said Kosch.

"No, no, you're staying deep," was again the response.

"Confidence was a lot of it," said Kosch. "Some days you feel faster than others, and it wasn't that I wasn't fast, but when a guy gets a step on you and you're the same speed, you don't gain it back. It was a catch-22 for me, and I was wondering how to deal with it. I wanted to get physical, come up there and bump him around a little bit, let him know I wasn't just going to stand around. But God, they would not let me. I didn't know anything about him particularly. My junior year we played our standard defense and had a good close game with them up in Lincoln. They had more running success against us in that game. It [the switch] was just a calculated risk, I guess. They came up with a game plan, and we ran it for three and a half quarters."

The Husker offensive coaches made one minor adjustment to their bread-and-butter play. "I don't recall the coaches being too worried about any particular Oklahoma defender," said Jeff Kinney. "We did make one adjustment at halftime. We moved the isolation hole off of the guard and moved it out one hole to the tackle. They were pinching down and kind of cutting things off, so in the second half I was going to read the tackle's block instead of the guards. We made the adjustment to move that read out one hole.

"We ran a lot of isolation plays off either one of the guards," said Kinney. "That was the hole you would attack. The fullback would read the guard's block and he would look for the linebacker. So what we ended up doing was just doing that off the tackle, and then I could break it either inside or outside. I broke it outside quite a few times in that second half.

"There were a few things said by Coach Devaney at halftime, but he didn't need to say a lot," continued Kinney. "I was surprised—maybe we all were—that Oklahoma moved the ball so well against our defense, because I knew from practicing against them how good our defense was. For us to see that happen we had to look at each other and say, 'You know, guys, we're going to have to score more points than they are.' The one thing that stuck in my mind, most of us knew that the whole season boiled down to the next half. We were all very determined to lay it all on the line. It was very real. We just decided they were not going to stop us. We were going to move the football. We didn't do a very good job of running the ball in the first half. And we knew that we had to control the football and score some points in the second half."

In the Oklahoma locker room, Fairbanks and his team were liking their chances. "We just wanted to continue running inside and misdirection plays. That was the biggest adjustment we made at halftime. And we wanted to try to take advantage of the fact that, for the most part, they were trying to cover our tight end and wide receiver with one player and we thought that we were going to win that match occasionally."

"We always had tremendous confidence," said Greg Pruitt. "We thought it would be a good close game in the second half, but we never thought that they could beat us. We thought that Tom [Brahaney] could handle Rich Glover by himself. And we found out that he needed help and gave it to him. But I was worried we were getting away too much from what we did best, and that's run the ball. They [coaches] felt that if Nebraska was going to key on me I was going to be a decoy, and we were going to pass off of them keying on me. I disagreed with that because I had been keyed on every week. Keying on me was one thing—stopping me entirely was another. I never carried the ball a lot. It didn't take me a lot of carries to get things done. If I was the coach, I'd have given the ball to Greg Pruitt some more. But I didn't ask them to do that because what we were doing was working and we were a team."

For the only time all season, Nebraska's primary ball handlers were wearing tear-away jerseys. They were noticeable because, unlike the standard-issue jerseys worn by the other Huskers, they lacked red stripes around the shoulders, and the fact that they were literally being shredded by Oklahoma's defenders every time they took hold of one. Jerry Tagge and Jeff Kinney in particular were doing a number on the tear-aways. Both went through all the disposable shirts on hand with their respective numbers, and by game's end each man was wearing a tattered rag and their shoulder pads were openly flopping about.

Kinney was pure Nebraska. Easy with a smile, married to his high school sweetheart from McCook, and determined. He wasn't the fastest or the strongest player on the field, but while *all* football players and teams tell themselves they are not going to be stopped, Jeff Kinney actually believed he could not be stopped. There's a difference, and Jeff Kinney was about to demonstrate it to a nationwide audience.

An offense that handled the ball as delicately as Oklahoma did was prone to fumbles, often by the bushel. As the second half got under way, Jack Mildren took a wicked hit from Nebraska defensive end John Adkins and put the ball on the carpet. Dave Mason, the monster (rover) in Nebraska's 5–2 defense, who was from the same Green Bay high school as Tagge and Jim Anderson, fell on the ball at midfield.

Four plays after the fumble, Tagge kept the ball on an option play and took it around the right end for 32 yards to the Oklahoma three-yard line. On the next play, Kinney crashed into the end zone behind the block of tackle Al Austin, completing a 53-yard drive.

Nebraska was back in front now 21–17 with 8:54 left in the third period, and the Husker offense seemed to be finding its stride. Tagge was throwing the occasional pass, but it was becoming evident that the Nebraska offense wanted to keep the ball out of the hands of the Oklahoma offense, and the way to do that was to run the ball.

Kinney got the chance to do so again almost immediately when Oklahoma was forced to punt after Mildren was tackled by end Willie Harper for a 12-yard loss. Using nine plays and nearly five minutes, the Husker offensive line root-hogged Oklahoma's defense and Nebraska moved the ball 61 yards for its fourth touchdown. For a brief moment, it appeared the Sooner defense might hold, but on third down Tagge threw to Johnny Rodgers at the one-yard line for the first down. On the next play, Kinney got behind Austin again, and tight end Jerry List, and bruised his way in for the score with 3:38 left in the third quarter.

The score was 28–17 in Nebraska's favor. In slightly more than eleven minutes, the Husker running game had imposed its will upon the game and the Sooner defenders. "They were more consistent and accurate, and their execution was better than anybody we had seen," said Oklahoma defensive back Steve O'Shaughnessy. "They had great athletes to go with that and they really didn't make mistakes. That was the difference. Not that their technique was different or what they did running or passing was anything exotic. They were just accurate, consistent, and mistakefree."

"Jeff Kinney ran very hard," said Lucious Selmon. "When I watched film of him, I used to think, 'I'm glad I wasn't at Oklahoma when Steve Owens was because that guy ran hard, and I'd hated to have been on the scout team and have him running into me all the time.' I kind of sized Kinney up as being that type of runner. Not quite as bruising as Steve, and a little shiftier. Very impressive. He ran the ball very, very hard. I remember trying to get off a block to tackle him, and I ended up hitting him right around his midsection and it just knocked the wind out of me. Luckily I was able to hang on until someone else got there, but if they hadn't gotten there quick he would have run right on through me. He was a very hard runner inside, and ran well on the perimeter, too. I have a photo of when he scored one of his touchdowns, and I'd gotten double-teamed and got my butt knocked back into the end zone, and Jeff Kinney is stepping right over the top of my head. He sure was on his game that day."

Everyone on the field that Thanksgiving Day gets a kick out of joking about the wobbly passes Jack Mildren supposedly threw. With time slipping away in the third quarter, no one expected to see Jon Harrison throw a wobbly pass of his own, let alone one that would yet again shift the momentum in the game.

With the ball on their own thirty-three-yard line, the Oklahoma staff called for a reverse pass, with Harrison doing the throwing to Albert Chandler. It was a play that would take advantage of the aggressive reads Jim Anderson was making playing over Chandler. "That was funny when that play came in," said Harrison. "We had a player named Willie Franklin who was second team behind me. He was the national junior college javelin thrower, and he could throw a really nice pass—far and a spiral and all that. We'd run that play in practice every once in a while, and when we did they'd have Willie come in and throw it. I was surprised when they called it, but figured I'd just heave it out there. Rich Glover hit me as soon as I threw it. It should have been a touchdown. Albert Chandler was open when I threw it, and it got to him, but he had to sort of stop to catch."

"We practiced against their reverse in practice," said Anderson. "Early in the season they had run that play by just running the ball. We ran that play in practice several times, as a run of course—they hadn't shown the pass yet. So, we practiced it as a run, and I remember talking about it in practice with Coach Powers and Kiffen and we hadn't seen any pass. We'd probably have been better off if we hadn't practiced it at all. As it was, I just played it as a run and Chandler just ran right by me. Then he got back behind Bill [Kosch] and I finally ran him down way downfield."

"We practiced against that end around," said Kosch, "and oh

God, I made a mistake. The whole point was that when he went on a reverse I was supposed to yell 'reverse' one time and take off on a forty-five-degree angle looking for the tight end. And I stood there for one more split second, because I yelled 'reverse' twice. That ruined the timing of the whole play defensively for us. I should have knocked the ball down because I got there just as he was catching the ball. If I would have broke after yelling one 'reverse,' I would have been there. And, dammit, he caught it. We're talking about microseconds. It wasn't a surprise, but I didn't break right away."

By the time Anderson and Kosch brought Chandler to the ground, he was on their sixteen-yard line. Mildren kept the ball on the next four plays, and with twenty-eight seconds left in the third period, he dragged linebacker Bill Terrio and monster back Dave Mason into the end zone.

The score now stood 28–24 in Nebraska's favor, and heading into the fourth quarter Husker fans could feel confident that the game was in the hands of their two old dependables, Jerry Tagge and Jeff Kinney.

Jerry Tagge's performance had been sneakily brilliant all day long. He had connected on a few key passes, but mostly what he'd done was outthought the Oklahoma defense and coaching staff. Immediately after the game, Chuck Fairbanks complimented Tagge on his intelligent use of "automatics," or checking off at the line of scrimmage to a play other than the one called in the huddle. Mostly, he was just changing what side Jeff Kinney ran to. "I just went up to the line and looked at where their safety was coming up," said Tagge. "Wherever he went, we went the other way."

Tagge had been the hero on the winning drive for the national championship against LSU, and the most reliable quarterback in the country all season long. He was the last person on the field anyone thought would goof up a play that could irrevocably change the tide of the game.

FOURTEEN

Time and I against any two.

—Spanish proverb

WITH THEIR FIRST POSSESSION OF THE FOURTH QUAR-
ter, the Nebraska Cornhuskers were once again pushing the ball
relentlessly down the field toward a score that would, in all proba-
bility, be the end of Oklahoma's chances for the Big Eight championship, an undefeated season, and the national championship.

The ball was on the Oklahoma thirty-one-yard line when Jerry
Tagge made a silly mistake attempting an unnecessary maneuver
with the ball on a fake end around to Johnny Rodgers. In an
attempt to increase the effectiveness of the feint, Tagge slipped the
ball behind his own back and attempted to grab it with his opposite hand. It wasn't a whimsical move on his part. "It's a better
fake," said Tagge. "I figured they'd key on Johnny Rodgers, so I
gave a good fake to him." He'd pulled off the behind-the-back routine earlier in the game without a hitch, and had also done it in the
Orange Bowl against LSU. With successful precedents, Tagge figured it was as safe as any other play.

What Tagge didn't allow for was that just as he was most vul-
nerable, with the ball behind his back, Sooner reserve linebacker
Danny Mullen would pop him one. The ball fluttered to the
ground, and Lucious Selmon covered it for Oklahoma.

The Sooners struck quickly when finally, after a day of being denied a breakout, Greg Pruitt broke loose for 18 yards to the Nebraska thirty-three. After chalking up one first down, Mildren and his crew faced a fourth and two at the twenty-one. A field goal to pull within a point was never a consideration, even though nearly nine minutes were left in the game. To give the ball back to Nebraska without at least having secured the lead was folly because Oklahoma might never see the ball again. Mildren ran the option and kept the ball, and made the first down.

After three more plays, the Sooners again faced fourth down. This time they needed seven yards with the ball on the sixteen. There was 7:10 remaining in the game when Mildren hoisted yet another pass toward Johnny Harrison, who had gotten behind Bill Kosch for one last time. The record crowd of 63,385 at Owen Field exploded. Incredibly, amazingly, and unbelievably, the Sooners had come from eleven points down to take the lead against a defense that had crushed every other opponent it faced all year.

"Nobody had scored on us like that," said Larry Jacobson. "It was a knockdown fight in the trenches. But the rivalry we had with Oklahoma was one of mutual respect. There was no cheap shots, no talking at all."

Exhausted, the Sooner offensive line retired to the bench after the extra point that put their team ahead 31–28. "We've got them now," Tom Brahaney recalled Dean Unruh saying to him.

"I remember," said Brahaney, "thinking immediately, 'Oh, God, I wish he hadn't said that.'"

The Nebraska offense was purpose-built for the task that it now faced: take the ball the length of the field and burn up what was left of the clock. The Oklahoma band played "Boomer Sooner" over and over again, and the crowd built up its throatiest chant of "Dee-fense! Dee-fense!!"

In the huddle, Tagge had the undivided attention of his team. "Nobody said a word but me," said Tagge. "We all knew what had to be done without saying a thing." Tagge eyeballed the Sooner safety on each play as he approached the line. The ball was going to Jeff Kinney, of that there was no doubt. It was just a matter of what direction Kinney would take it.

"They had just gone ahead of us," said Kinney, "and we got in the huddle and Jerry said, 'We know what we gotta do. We have to score.' Very matter of fact, no screaming and yelling. I think I got the ball every play except two or three times on that drive. I was used to carrying the ball twenty or twenty-five times a game."

On third and one from their own thirty-five, Tagge pitched the ball to Kinney. It was an unexpected call on a down and distance that seemed to cry out for the Huskers' go-to short-yardage play, the isolation. Instead, Kinney swung wide for the corner, and once into the open field broke three separate tackles while picking up 17 yards. "My legs cramped up after that and I had to come out for a couple of plays," said Kinney. "And they were rubbing them down and got me back up and I said, 'Coach, I'm ready to go back in.' It was third and eight."

The ball was on the Oklahoma forty-six-yard line and there was 4:30 left on the clock. It was *the* critical play in the game, a fact that escaped no one. Tagge rolled out to his right, looking for someone—anyone—to throw the ball to. For a split instant, it looked as if Tagge would be tackled. Raymond Hamilton, Oklahoma's star defensive lineman, appeared to have Tagge cornered. "Raymond Hamilton and Derland Moore both played hurt during the game," said Fairbanks. "You're talking about two outstanding players who played nine or ten years in the pros. Raymond had a turf-toe injury, which made it difficult to change direction. On that third down and long yardage we took a time-out and called a blitz that freed Raymond Hamilton to get to the passer, but he missed the tackle on Tagge because of his inability to change direction. That allowed Jerry to get free. That was the biggest play in the game other than Rodgers running the punt back."

"It was our best defensive player against their best offensive player," said Sooner defensive coordinator Larry Lacewell after the game. "If Tagge doesn't get the most valuable player at their banquet, then it's fixed."

Saved by turf toe, Tagge drilled a low pass to Rodgers, who was sinking to his knees between defenders at the Oklahoma thirty-five. "I would have had to walk to the Oklahoma side if I dropped that," said Rodgers. "I wouldn't have had any friends left. It was low, but not hard to catch as long as I concentrated." Rodgers said he was bumped by Sooner defensive back Kenith Pope at the line "and when that happens, Jerry knows I break the pattern. He knew I'd be there somewhere."

"I was starting to turn up the field to run," said Tagge. "That's when I saw Johnny Rodgers run across the field. It was a poor pass, good catch. That was the biggest play of the game. We sent four receivers out and they were supposed to hook twelve or fourteen yards deep. I was supposed to read the middle linebacker. Whichever way he went, I would throw the other way. But he went straight back and Oklahoma had everybody and his sister back there in the hook zone."

"We had everybody covered," said Steve O'Shaugnessy. "I played the entire game from start to finish. It was as electric as you can imagine. There are several plays in the game which you could say if that didn't happen the outcome would be different. This is one of those. Not as exciting as the runback on the punt by Rodgers, but it was important scoring that first down because they were driving with seven minutes left."

"Oh, I thought we had 'em on third and eight," said Lucious Selmon. "Raymond Hamilton was just about to get there, but couldn't put enough pressure on his foot to get there with the explosiveness he needed. If we had stopped them then, they probably would have gone for it on fourth. Not to say we would have stopped them, but it was an awfully big sequence of events."

On the next play, his legs refreshed, Kinney took a handoff, cut outside and mowed down a disheartened group of Sooner defenders on his way to 13 more yards. The assault was relentless and brutal, and with just under two minutes left, the Huskers had the ball on the six-yard line. Kinney had carried it five times for 46 yards.

Tagge called time-out and headed to the sidelines to talk with Devaney.

"I know we can score, coach, but I'm worried about eating up time," Tagge said.

"We're going for the touchdown," said Devaney. "There won't be any ties."

"We'll get it," said Tagge.

"What's your best play?" said Devaney.

"I think it's the left off-tackle with Jeff."

"OK," said Devaney, "let's run it without any mistakes."

Kinney got the call and plowed into the left side of the line behind Daryl White for 4 yards. In the commotion, the Sooners believed Kinney fumbled and that Raymond Hamilton had recovered the ball. The referees ruled the ball dead.

"We thought we had the fumble," said Selmon. "Kinney had the ball, they were running pretty much to the outside butt of the left offensive guard, and there was a scramble for the ball. To this day I never heard of that kind of call before. It wasn't a call that he was down; they just said the whistle had blown. It was really one that we stood out there and complained about when we probably should have went ahead and shut up and got lined up and played the next down. It was something we let stick in our craw. We thought it was the second bad call against us. We thought there was a clip on that play [Johnny Rodgers' punt return]. It was a little bit of a distraction."

With 1:38 left on the clock, Kinney followed fullback Maury Damkroger into the end zone, and Nebraska took the lead for the final time, 35–31.

"One thing that sticks out in my mind after Jeff Kinney scored the winning touchdown: There was no tumultuous celebrations after like there are today after a team scores a touchdown," said Mike Beran, who was watching from the sidelines. "I think the fullback, Maury Damkroger, went over to give Jeff a quick hug, and everyone else just got up and went to the huddle to score the extra point. Just another day at the ranch; that's what you're supposed to do."

Jack Mildren and the Sooners had ninety-eight seconds to pull out a miracle. "Toward the end of the game, they let Jon Harrison get behind them. He came open and Jack overthrew him by maybe a foot," said Leon Crosswhite. "He'd have gone all the way. I'm fifty-two years old, and I can still see that plain as day."

"It was still real tense, because they had the ball and enough time to score," said Jim Anderson. "And there was one famous play in there where Mildren let the ball fly to Harrison and Joe [Blahak] was over there covering him and he was still open. I was on the other side of the field, and watched it just sail over Harrison's arms. I was never so glad to see anything hit the ground in my life. Talk about a sigh of relief. It was one of those life-passing-before-your-eyes kind of things. I was over on Chandler and I saw the throw, and I saw Harrison running free and the ball sail over his arms. If that play was complete the whole end could have been different."

"At some point we switched back to our regular positions," said Bill Kosch. "I don't know exactly why they changed back. I do remember they ran a post corner pattern on Joe [Blahak] and he came back laughing and said, 'I was beat.' I think Harrison would say if he just could have caught that pass they would have won. But Jack overthrew that one."

"I still dream about that last throw," said Harrison. "We were going to get the ball a last time, and I figured they'd go into some sort of zone or prevent. But they didn't, they just stayed man-to-man. And I ran a move and I barely bumped Blahak and it made me go a little more into the middle of the field, and I couldn't get back out to the ball. I would have scored if I caught up to it, but I didn't get by him clean. I don't think about plays that I made, like the touchdowns I scored against Nebraska. The ones that bother me are the plays I didn't make. You don't get too many opportunities like winning a state championship or a national championship, and when you don't take advantage of it . . ."

Facing fourth and forever, Mildren dropped back to pass one more time, but was immediately pressured by Larry Jacobson. "On the last play, I rushed in and he faked me out," said Jacobson. "I went rolling on the ground, and Rich [Glover] came in and knocked the ball down on the pass. That was the end of the game. Jack Mildren played a hell of a game."

It was Oklahoma's Larry Lacewell who summed up the end of the game best. "They got last bats," said Lacewell.

One writer covering the game wrote, "At the finish, the record crowd at Owen Field was limp. Spectators and participants alike sensed they had witnessed an unforgettable game. The incomparable game."

Today Jon Harrison coaches the receivers at Abilene Cooper. "When I started coaching, I was pretty little," said Harrison. "Most of the kids didn't believe I could play for OU because I was so small. And I'd show 'em the films and they couldn't believe it. The game gets bigger and bigger as it gets farther away. I'll be walking down the hall in school and someone will say the game was on. I just wish we would have won instead of lost."

"You score thirty-one points against a great Nebraska defense and you think you've done well," said Barry Switzer. "But if I had called six or seven more passes that day to Jon Harrison, on run-down situations, we would have won the game by two or three touchdowns. I really believe that. Jon Harrison may have been the most underrated player we ever had at Oklahoma."

"Bob Devaney came up behind me after the game," said Bill Kosch, "and put his arm around my shoulder and looked me in the eye and said, 'Billy, I apologize for putting you out of position.' I said, 'That's OK. We won the game.' I wasn't going to say anything other than that. The objective was complete. We won, even if we lost some battles out there. Warren Powers kind of said the same thing to me. I just laugh about it today. That's all you can do.

"Joe [Blahak] and I are still best friends. We don't bring it up. It's just something we know. We don't have to talk about it because we know. But we talk to other people about it."

"My grandpa always used to tell me you can find something good in any tragedy," said Greg Pruitt. "Now, I'm not saying losing a football game is a tragedy, but it was as far as we were concerned. All our hopes—we lost one game, we lost everything as a result of it—the national championship and the Big Eight championship.

"I've always told people that I felt like in that game, we just happened to be behind when the clock ran out," said Pruitt. "We both had superior offenses. They probably had a slight edge on us defensively, but neither defense could really stop either offense. They just did a little better job. But if you take away the punt return, we win the game. It was our special teams that didn't really execute that cost us the game. And I made the number one mistake. If I'd just done what they taught us . . . I later on became a punt returner in the National Football League, and anytime anybody made that same mistake I made I'd make them pay.

"I think we hurried up and got off the field. We were probably a little bit shocked. We really didn't think we could lose. It was a great game, but that doesn't mean much right after you lose. Later on, after I was in the pros, people started to talk about it as the greatest football game ever. A game where number one and number two met and it lived up to all the expectations. I never accepted it as a defeat," said Pruitt, laughing. "I always say if we had gotten the ball just one more time . . ."

"After the game I told our players that they were privileged to have earned the right to play in a game of that magnitude," said Chuck Fairbanks. "And they should always be proud of it. They don't ever have to hang their head about it. It didn't work out right, but it wasn't because they didn't try hard. They can look on that game forever and ever, as I do, that we were fortunate to be in it. I can't count the times people have asked me about the game, but I don't begrudge people asking about it."

"One thing I do remember," said Jack Mildren, "was that after we went for it on fourth down at the end of the game and didn't get it, Nebraska took the ball over on our twenty-yard line. Now, in today's era, some teams would have tried to score again. That's very classless in my judgment. Nebraska didn't do that. The field was a madhouse. It was very disappointing to play as well as we did and lose. Yet, on the other side, kind of hard to argue with facts such as they were. We had our chances. We didn't leave anything in our pockets, we left it all out there. Which is different than some earlier number one versus number two games. But to say as a twenty-one-year-old kid that it's not disappointing when you've always wanted to play for a national championship . . . it was gone, that was it. That part was tough."

"Not to make this into a soap opera," said Mildren, "but we've come to know those [Nebraska] guys over the years and we gained great respect for them. I never dreamed we'd still be talking about it more than thirty years later. Gracious me.

"After the game, Fairbanks was doing his weekly show on top of the open-air press box. This was a special show that was taped for a statewide audience. All of a sudden the phone rings. The phone isn't supposed to ring when he's doing his show. That's bad news. He was clearly irritated. 'Don't tell me there's a phone call. I'm trying to do the show and get out of here.' Then I hear him say, 'Yes, Mr. President . . .' That was an important deal when the president calls."

"Until the final gun sounded I never thought we'd lose," said Dean Unruh. "Until time ran out and the game was over, I was confident we were going to win. I don't think anyone thought we were going to beat Nebraska 50–0, but we felt we'd win. We knew Nebraska was going to score, and we knew we could score on them. We thought if we played hard for sixty minutes the game would take care of itself. But certainly no one thought we were going to walk all over Nebraska. I also believe everyone in our locker room thought we would win, that we were the better team. We knew we would be challenged, but we weren't overly concerned like, 'What are we going to do?' For a lot of us, that's what we came to play for.

"I was devastated at the end. You work for however long you work. Whether you go back to the final game in high school, and you're looking at three years' worth of work to get in that situation, and to fall short, I was devastated. I remember walking off the field with Albert Chandler. We were speechless. It was a hard loss to take. It really sat sideways with me. And to be honest, I've never watched the game in its entirety. We did not watch the game film with the coaches like we always did. We had Sunday off. Got up and ran, didn't watch film. We never as an offensive team watched the Nebraska film. I think I was five or six years out of college and I was having a business lunch and someone said to me, 'You played in the 1971 OU–Nebraska game, didn't you? That was a great game.' And I said, 'Yeah, that was a great game.' And that was the first time I really appreciated the fact that I got to play in that game. Up till then, I always thought about the bitterness of losing—of not winning that game. And since that time, I wouldn't trade playing in that game for anything."

"I never saw the game until about two years ago some guy in Midland had a recording of it from the TV broadcast," said Tom Brahaney. "So I watched it and I remembered how we all thought Nebraska's guys were big—real big, a lot bigger than ours. And watching that recording of the game, we looked like a bunch of ants out there. We were midgets compared to what they are now."

"After the game was over," said John Carroll, "Coach Fairbanks said, good game, hate to see somebody lose, we'll see you tomorrow. That Sunday we went back ready for the film and we got in there and he said, 'Put your stuff on, go loosen up; we're not going to watch this film. There's no reason to.' He didn't want to bring back the bad taste in our mouth. So we never did see the game film. I didn't really get to see the game until ten or twelve years later when my parents gave me a tape of the game. It was the game of the century. You don't get to play in too many of those."

"I don't think I had been, up to that time, that depressed in my life," said Steve O'Shaughnessy. "I was on the verge of tears. My older sister, Karen, lived in Mexico and she came up for the game. It was the first and last game that she ever saw and I apologized to her. I said we hadn't lost one all year and you come to this and look what happens. It was very depressing. It was surreal because we said, 'We couldn't have lost, something's wrong here, this must be a bad dream.' "

"We got the ball back at the very end of the game and had to run the clock out," said Jeff Kinney. "The memory that I have is of the crowd storming the field. Amidst that sea of humanity the first person I ran into was my father. He got the rest of my jersey that was left on me, and that was kind of neat. He must have known where I was because I had no idea . . .

"This game, the next day, took on a life of its own. And just got bigger and bigger and bigger. Oklahoma was a great football team. They went down [to the Sugar Bowl] and beat Auburn really, really bad."

"After the game, I remember everyone throwing everyone in the showers," said Larry Jacobson. "And I remember the plane couldn't get to the terminal. There were 30,000 people there. They had to let us out to get on buses. The whole route to the airport—and it was only two or three miles—but it was just packed with people who were going nuts. After the game we went down and hit a couple of bars and we didn't have to buy any drinks all night."

"Yes sir, Mr. President. They sold a lot of popcorn today. Nobody left." So said Bob Devaney on the phone to President Richard Nixon from the Nebraska locker room.

"I've never been in a game where it seemed like the time went by so fast," said Leon Crosswhite. "I felt like I blinked and it was over."

"I can't think of another game where people still talk about the team that lost," said Jerry Tagge. "Even the losers were heroes in that game."

"Well, obviously we were ecstatic," said Jim Anderson. "After this thing had been built up all that time, and we were playing down there [Oklahoma], I think we all sensed that we experienced something special. I showered up and got dressed a little early and I went back up in the stadium. I went up into the stands, and it was totally empty. Everybody had gone, it was quiet. I just went up there and looked down at the field, and just tried to soak up the moment and capture that feeling in my memory. And it worked. I remember it like it was yesterday.

"I grew up in Green Bay and I had seen some old Marlboro commercials of Paul Hornung reminiscing, looking over a field. As a kid we grew up with the Packers and I had seen that commercial so many times I think it stuck in my head. And that's how I got the idea to go up there all by myself and stop and smell the roses. It

174

was just a quiet moment, and I tried to savor that moment in feeling. I wasn't picturing any players, although that's what he did in the commercial. I was trying to savor the moment and capture the feeling for myself."

Said Lyell Bremser, "I never thought I would live this long to see this kind of a football game."

Team Statistics

	NEBRASKA	OKLAHOMA
Points	35	31
First downs	19	22
Rushes/yards	59/297	64/279
Passing yards	65	188
Punt/kick return yards	80	7
Interceptions	0	0
Fumbles lost	1	3
Yards penalized	5	0

Individual Statistics

Nebraska

RUSHING

	ATTEMPTS	YARDS	TD
Kinney	31	174	4
Tagge	17	49	0
Rodgers	4	27	0
Damkroger	3	23	0
Dixon	1	2	0
Olds	4	22	0

PASSING

	ATTEMPTS	COMPLETE	YARDS	TD
Tagge	12	6	65	0

RECEIVING

	NO.	YARDS	TD
Rodgers	5	61	0
Kinney	1	4	0

Oklahoma

RUSHING

	ATTEMPTS	YARDS	TD
Mildren	31	130	2
Crosswhite	12	59	0
Pruitt	10	53	0
Welch	8	26	0
Wylie	3	11	0

PASSING

	ATTEMPTS	COMPLETE	YARDS	TD
Mildren	10	5	137	2
Harrison	1	1	51	0

RECEIVING

	NO.	YARDS	TD
Harrison	4	115	2
Chandler	2	73	0

Following the game of the century, both Nebraska and Oklahoma won their final regular-season games. Nebraska beat Hawaii, and Oklahoma beat Oklahoma State. On New Year's Day 1972, Oklahoma thrashed Auburn in the Sugar Bowl by a score of 40–22.

That night, Nebraska faced undefeated Alabama in the Orange Bowl. Alabama was coached by Devaney's old nemesis, Bear Bryant. Alabama, too, ran the wishbone. "They didn't stand a chance against us," said Monte Kiffin.

"It wasn't even a game," said Larry Jacobson.

Nebraska won, 38–6, completing a perfect 12–0 season. For the second year in a row, Nebraska was the national champion.

Oklahoma finished number two in the polls.

Bob Devaney coached one more season before stepping aside to become full-time athletic director at Nebraska. His record as Nebraska's head coach was 101–20–2. Tom Osborne, Devaney's hand-chosen successor, served as head coach for twenty-five years, with a record of 255–49–3.

Barry Switzer became the head coach of the Oklahoma Sooners in 1973. Over sixteen seasons using solely the wishbone offense, he compiled a record of 157–29.

ACKNOWLEDGMENTS

The author is indebted to the following people for graciously offering their time for interviews: Leon Crosswhite, Boyd Epley, Chuck Fairbanks, Don Jimerson, Merv Johnson, Jeff Kinney, Jack Mildren, Greg Pruitt, Lucious Selmon, Barry Switzer, Dean Unruh, Jim Anderson, Mike Beran, Tom Brahaney, John Carroll, Jon Harrison, Larry Jacobson, Monte Kiffin, Bill Kosch, Steve O'Shaughnessy, and Neil Amdur.

Remarkable assistance during research and interviews was selflessly offered by Seamus McGraw, John Ledesma, Rebecca Swanner, Jonathan Stern, Joseph Passov, and Angela Corcoran. The librarian at the *Lincoln Journal Star*, Mary Jo Bratton, was extraordinarily helpful. Kenny Mossman, the sports information director at the University of Oklahoma, was generous with his precious time. At the University of Nebraska, Chris Anderson and her staff were helpful.

My dear friend Randy Voorhees was the inspiration behind this book. Mike Hammer, one of the all-time great guys, provided encouragement when it was desperately needed.

At Simon & Schuster, Tara Parsons was a godsend.

From days long, long ago, and time spent with me either in person or in spirit on football fields across the country, the following were frequently in my thoughts during this writing: Tex Flannery, Rev. Anthony Orth, Rich Kelly, Skip Duffy, Joe Franchella, Bill Von Leer, Ted Steingraber, Tim Steigerwalt, Tony Casselli, Kevin Taylor, Nick DiMaria, Mike Carroll, Dave Murphy, John DiGregorio, Bobby Gagliardi, Marty Geisler, Gil Crews, Lee Roberts, Earl Cleghorn, Nick Rapone, Paul Davis, Joe Moore, and Bruce Arians.

INDEX

ABOUT THE AUTHOR

MICHAEL CORCORAN has written seven previous books, including *Duel in the Sun,* an account of the 1977 British Open, and *For Which It Stands: An Anecdotal Biography of the American Flag.* He has written for numerous magazines and been the editor of a few. He lives with his wife and their children in Springtown, Pennsylvania.